IN A MARINE LIGHT

Raymond Carver was born in 1939. He was a
Guggenheim Fellow in 1979 and was twice awarded grants
by the National Endowment for the Arts. He taught
at the University of Iowa, the University of Texas, and
the University of California. His three collections of
poetry and books of short stories, including *Fires* and
The Stories of Raymond Carver, are also available in
Picador.

Raymond Carver died in 1988.

Also by Raymond Carver in Picador

Fires

The Stories of Raymond Carver

Raymond Carver

IN A MARINE LIGHT

SELECTED POEMS

published by Pan Books
in association with Collins Harvill

The poems in this collection were first
published in volume form in *Where Water Comes
Together with Other Water* and *Ultramarine* by
Random House, Inc.

Grateful acknowledgement is made to the
following publications in which some of the
poems in this book originally appeared:
*The Atlantic, Crazy Horse, Grand Street, New
Letters, The New York Times Magazine, The
New Yorker, Northwest Review, The Ohio
Review, The Ontario Review, The Paris Review,
Ploughshares, Poetry, Seneca Review, Tendril,
TriQuarterly, Zyzyva*, and in limited editions
from William B. Ewert, Publisher.

First published by Collins Harvill
This picador edition published 1988 by Pan Books Ltd,
Cavaye Place, London SW10 9PG
9 8 7 6 5 4 3 2
© Raymond Carver 1984, 1985, 1986, 1987, 1988
ISBN 0 330 30307 4
Printed and bound in Great Britain by
Richard Clay Ltd, Bungay, Suffolk

Tess Gallagher

Light in my being, light in the kitchen,
evening light, morning light.
Light between despair and luminosity . . .
The nets that wavered in the light
keep on shining from the sea.

Pablo Neruda, *Isla Negra*

CONTENTS

THREE

SIX

In A Marine Light

ONE

HAPPINESS

So early it's still almost dark out.
I'm near the window with coffee,
and the usual early morning stuff
that passes for thought.
When I see the boy and his friend
walking up the road
to deliver the newspaper.
They wear caps and sweaters,
and one boy has a bag over his shoulder.
They are so happy
they aren't saying anything, these boys.
I think if they could, they would take
each other's arm.
It's early in the morning,
and they are doing this thing together.
They come on, slowly.
The sky is taking on light,
though the moon still hangs pale over the water.
Such beauty that for a minute
death and ambition, even love,
doesn't enter into this.
Happiness. It comes on
unexpectedly. And goes beyond, really,
any early morning talk about it.

THE PROJECTILE

for Haruki Murakami

We sipped tea. Politely musing
on possible reasons for the success
of my books in your country. Slipped
into talk of pain and humiliation
you find occurring, and reoccurring,
in my stories. And that element
of sheer chance. How all this translates
in terms of sales.
I looked into a corner of the room.
And for a minute I was 16 again,
careening around in the snow
in a '50 Dodge sedan with five or six
bozos. Giving the finger
to some other bozos, who yelled and pelted
our car with snowballs, gravel, old
tree branches. We spun away, shouting.
And we were going to leave it at that.
But my window was down three inches.
Only three inches. I hollered out
one last obscenity. And saw this guy
wind up to throw. From this vantage,
now, I imagine I see it coming. See it
speeding through the air while I watch,
like those soldiers in the first part
of the last century watched canisters
of shot fly in their direction
while they stood, unable to move
for the dread fascination of it.
But I *didn't* see it. I'd already turned
my head to laugh with my pals.

16

When something slammed into the side
of my head so hard it broke my eardrum and fell
in my lap, intact. A ball of packed ice
and snow. The pain was stupendous.
And the humiliation.
It was awful when I began to weep
in front of those tough guys while they
cried, *Dumb luck. Freak accident.*
A chance in a million!
The guy who threw it, he had to be amazed
and proud of himself while he took
the shouts and backslaps of the others.
He must have wiped his hands on his pants.
And messed around a little more
before going home to supper. He grew up
to have his share of setbacks and got lost
in his life, same as I got lost in mine.
He never gave that afternoon
another thought. And why should he?
So much else to think about always.
Why remember that stupid car sliding
down the road, then turning the corner
and disappearing?
We politely raise our teacups in the room.
A room that for a minute something else entered.

WOOLWORTH'S, 1954

Where this floated up from, or why,
I don't know. But thinking about this
since just after Robert called
telling me he'd be here in a few minutes
to go clamming.

How on my first job I worked
under a man named Sol.
Fifty-some years old, but
a stockboy like I was.
Had worked his way
up to nothing. But grateful
for his job, same as me.
He knew everything there was
to know about that dime-store
merchandise and was willing
to show me. I was sixteen, working
for six bits an hour. Loving it
that I was. Sol taught me
what he knew. He was patient,
though it helped I learned fast.

Most important memory
of that whole time: opening
the cartons of women's lingerie.
Underpants, and soft, clingy things
like that. Taking it out
of cartons by the handful. Something
sweet and mysterious about those
things even then. Sol called it

"linger-ey." "Linger-ey?"
What did I know? I called it
that for a while, too. "Linger-ey."

Then I got older. Quit being
a stockboy. Started pronouncing
that frog word right.
I knew what I was talking about!
Went to taking girls out
in hopes of touching that softness,
slipping down those underpants.
And sometimes it happened. God,
they let me. And they *were*
linger-ey, those underpants.
They tended to linger a little
sometimes, as they slipped down
off the belly, clinging lightly
to the hot white skin..
Passing over the hips and buttocks
and beautiful thighs, traveling
faster now as they crossed the knees,
the calves! Reaching the ankles,
brought together for this
occasion. And kicked free
onto the floor of the car and
forgotten about. Until you had
to look for them.

"Linger-ey."

Those sweet girls!
"Linger a little, for thou art fair."
I know who said that. It fits,
and I'll use it. Robert and his
kids and I out there on the flats

with our buckets and shovels.
His kids, who won't eat clams, cutting
up the whole time, saying "Yuck"
or "Ugh" as clams turned
up in the shovels full of sand
and were tossed into the bucket.
Me thinking all the while
of those early days in Yakima.
And smooth-as-silk underpants.
The lingering kind that Jeanne wore,
and Rita, Muriel, Sue, and her sister
Cora Mae. All those girls.
Grownup now. Or worse.
I'll say it: dead.

BALSA WOOD

My dad is at the stove in front of a pan with brains
and eggs. But who has any appetite
this morning? I feel flimsy as
balsa wood. Something has just been said.
My mom said it. What was it? Something,
I'll bet, that bears on money. I'll do my part
if I don't eat. Dad turns his back on the stove.
"I'm in a hole. Don't dig me deeper."
Light leaks in from the window. Someone's crying.
The last thing I recall is the smell
of burned brains and eggs. The whole morning
is shoveled into the garbage and mixed
with other things. Sometime later
he and I drive to the dump, ten miles out.
We don't talk. We throw our bags and cartons
onto a dark mound. Rats screech.
They whistle as they crawl out of rotten sacks
dragging their bellies. We get back in the car
to watch the smoke and fire. The motor's running.
I smell the airplane glue on my fingers.
He looks at me as I bring my fingers to my nose.
Then looks away again, toward town.
He wants to say something but can't.
He's a million miles away. We're both far away
from there, and still someone's crying. Even then
I was beginning to understand how it's possible
to be in one place. And someplace else, too.

SHIFTLESS

The people who were better than us were *comfortable*.
They lived in painted houses with flush toilets.
Drove cars whose year and make were recognizable.
The ones worse off were *sorry* and didn't work.
Their strange cars sat on blocks in dusty yards.
The years go by and everything and everyone
gets replaced. But this much is still true –
I never liked work. My goal was always
to be shiftless. I saw the merit in that.
I liked the idea of sitting in a chair
in front of your house for hours, doing nothing
but wearing a hat and drinking cola.
What's wrong with that?
Drawing on a cigarette from time to time.
Spitting. Making things out of wood with a knife.
Where's the harm there? Now and then calling
the dogs to hunt rabbits. Try it sometime.
Once in a while hailing a fat, blond kid like me
and saying, "Don't I know you?"
Not, "What are you going to be when you grow up?"

SON

Awakened this morning by a voice from my childhood
that says *Time to get up*, I get up.
All night long, in my sleep, trying
to find a place where my mother could live
and be happy. *If you want me to lose my mind*,
the voice says *okay. Otherwise,*
get me out of here! I'm the one to blame
for moving her to this town she hates. Renting
her the house she hates.
Putting those neighbors she hates so close.
Buying the furniture she hates.
Why didn't you give me money instead, and let me spend it?
I want to go back to California, the voice says.
I'll die if I stay here. Do you want me to die?
There's no answer to this, or to anything else
in the world this morning. The phone rings
and rings. I can't go near it for fear
of hearing my name once more. The same name
my father answered to for 53 years.
Before going to his reward.
He died just after saying "Take this
into the kitchen, son."
The word *son* issuing from his lips.
Wobbling in the air for all to hear.

MONEY

In order to be able to live
on the right side of the law.
To always use his own name
and phone number. To go bail
for a friend and not give
a damn if the friend skips town.
Hope, in fact, she does.
To give some money
to his mother. And to his
children and their mother.
Not save it. He wants
to use it up before it's gone.
Buy clothes with it.
Pay the rent and utilities.
Buy food, and then some.
Go out for dinner when he feels like it.
And it's okay
to order anything off the menu!
Buy drugs when he wants.
Buy a car. If it breaks
down, repair it. Or else
buy another. See that
boat? He might buy one
just like it. And sail it
around the Horn, looking
for company. He knows a girl
in Porto Alegre who'd love
to see him in
his own boat, sails full,
turn into the harbor for her.

A fellow who could afford
to come all this way
to see her. Just because
he liked the sound
of her laughter,
and the way she swings her hair.

THE MEADOW

In the meadow this afternoon, I fetch
any number of crazy memories. That
undertaker asking my mother did she
want to buy the entire suit to bury my dad in,
or just the coat? I don't
have to provide the answer to this,
or anything else. But, hey, he went
into the furnace wearing his britches.

This morning I looked at his picture.
Big, heavyset guy in the last year
of his life. Holding a monster salmon
in front of the shack where he lived
in Fortuna, California. My dad.
He's nothing now. Reduced to a cup of ashes,
and some tiny bones. No way
is this any way
to end your life as a man.
Though as Hemingway correctly pointed out,
all stories, if continued far enough,
end in death. Truly.

Lord, it's almost fall.
A flock of Canada geese passes
high overhead. The little mare lifts
her head, shivers once, goes back
to grazing. I think I will lie down
in this sweet grass. I'll shut my eyes
and listen to wind, and the sound of wings.

Just dream for an hour, glad to be here
and not there. There's that. But also
the terrible understanding
that men I loved have left
for some other, lesser place.

IN A MARINE LIGHT NEAR
SEQUIM, WASHINGTON

The green fields were beginning. And the tall, white
farmhouses after the tidal flats and those little sand crabs
that were ready to run, or else turn and square off, if
we moved the rock they lived under. The languor
of that subdued afternoon. The beauty of driving
that country road. Talking of Paris, our Paris.
And then you finding that place in the book
and reading to me about Anna Akhmatova's stay there with
   Modigliani.
Them sitting on a bench in the Luxembourg Gardens
under his enormous old black umbrella
reciting Verlaine to each other. Both of them
"as yet untouched by their futures." When
out in the field we saw
a bare-chested young man with his trousers rolled up,
like an ancient oarsman. He looked at us without curiosity.
Stood there and gazed indifferently.
Then turned his back to us and went on with his work.
As we passed like a beautiful black scythe
through that perfect landscape.

A WALK

I took a walk on the railroad track.
Followed that for a while
and got off at the country graveyard
where a man sleeps between
two wives. Emily van der Zee,
Loving Wife and Mother,
is at John van der Zee's right.
Mary, the second Mrs van der Zee,
also a Loving Wife, to his left.
First Emily went, then Mary.
After a few years, the old fellow himself.
Eleven children came from these unions.
And they, too, would all have to be dead now.
This is a quiet place. As good a place as any
to break my walk, sit, and provide against
my own death, which comes on.
But I don't understand, and I don't understand.
All I know about this fine, sweaty life,
my own or anyone else's,
is that in a little while I'll rise up
and leave this astonishing place
that gives shelter to dead people. This graveyard.
And go. Walking first on one rail
and then the other.

MY DAD'S WALLET

Long before he thought of his own death,
my dad said he wanted to lie close
to his parents. He missed them so
after they went away.
He said this enough that my mother remembered,
and I remembered. But when the breath
left his lungs and all signs of life
had faded, he found himself in a town
512 miles away from where he wanted most to be.

My dad, though. He was restless
even in death. Even in death
he had this one last trip to take.
All his life he liked to wander,
and now he had one more place to get to.

The undertaker said he'd arrange it,
not to worry. Some poor light
from the window fell on the dusty floor
where we waited that afternoon
until the man came out of the back room
and peeled off his rubber gloves.
He carried the smell of formaldehyde with him.
He was a big man, this undertaker said.
Then began to tell us why
he liked living in this small town.
This man who'd just opened my dad's veins.
How much is it going to cost? I said.

He took out his pad and pen and began
to write. First, the preparation charges.

Then he figured the transportation
of the remains at 22 cents a mile.
But this was a round-trip for the undertaker,
don't forget. Plus, say, six meals
and two nights in a motel. He figured
some more. Add a surcharge of
$210 for his time and trouble,
and there you have it.

He thought we might argue.
There was a spot of color on
each of his cheeks as he looked up
from his figures. The same poor light
fell in the same poor place on
the dusty floor. My mother nodded
as if she understood. But she
hadn't understood a word of it.
None of it had made any sense to her,
beginning with the time she left home
with my dad. She only knew
that whatever was happening
was going to take money.
She reached into her purse and brought up
my dad's wallet. The three of us
in that little room that afternoon.
Our breath coming and going.

We stared at the wallet for a minute.
Nobody said anything.
All the life had gone out of that wallet.
It was old and rent and soiled.
But it was my dad's wallet. And she opened
it and looked inside. Drew out
a handful of money that would go
toward this last, most astounding, trip.

31

TO BEGIN WITH

He took a room in a port city with a fellow
called Sulieman A. Sulieman and his wife,
an American known only as Bonnie. One thing
he remembered about his stay there
was how every evening Sulieman rapped
at his own front door before entering.
Saying, "Right, hello. Sulieman here."
After that, Sulieman taking off his shoes.
Putting pita bread and hummus into his mouth
in the company of his sullen wife.
Sometimes there was a piece of chicken
followed by cucumbers and tomatoes.
Then they all watched what passed for TV
in that country. Bonnie sitting in a chair
to herself, raving against the Jews.
At eleven o'clock she would say, "We have to sleep now."

But once they left their bedroom door open.
And he saw Sulieman make his bed on the floor
beside the big bed where Bonnie lay
and looked down at her husband.
They said something to each other in a foreign language.
Sulieman arranged his shoes by his head.
Bonnie turned off the light, and they slept.
But the man in the room at the back of the house
couldn't sleep at all. It was as if
he didn't believe in sleep any longer.
Sleep had been all right, once, in its time.
But it was different now.

Lying there at night, eyes open, arms at his sides,
his thoughts went out to his wife,
and his children, and everything that bore
on that leave-taking. Even the shoes
he'd been wearing when he left his house
and walked out. They were the real betrayers,
he decided. They'd brought him all this way
without once trying to do anything to stop him.
Finally, his thoughts came back to this room
and this house. Where they belonged.
Where he knew he was home.
Where a man slept on the floor of his own bedroom.
A man who knocked at the door of his own house,
announcing his meager arrival. Sulieman.
Who entered his house only after knocking
and then to eat pita bread and tomatoes
with his bitter wife. But in the course of those long nights
he began to envy Sulieman a little.
Not much, but a little. And so what if he did!
Sulieman sleeping on his bedroom floor.
But Sulieman sleeping in the same room,
at least, as his wife.

Maybe it was all right if she snored
and had blind prejudices. She wasn't so bad-
looking, that much was true, and if
Sulieman woke up he could at least
hear her from his place. Know she was there.
There might even be nights when he could reach
over and touch her through the blanket
without waking her. Bonnie. His wife.

Maybe in this life it was necessary to learn
to pretend to be a dog and sleep on the floor
in order to get along. Sometimes

33

this might be necessary. Who knows
anything these days?

At least it was a new idea and something,
he thought, he might have to try and understand.
Outside, the moon reached over the water
and disappeared finally. Footsteps

moved slowly down the street and came to a stop
outside his window. The streetlight
went out, and the steps passed on.
The house became still and, in one way at least,
like all the other houses – totally dark.
He held onto his blanket and stared at the ceiling.
He had to start over. To begin with –
the oily smell of the sea, the rotting tomatoes.

THIS MORNING

This morning was something. A little snow
lay on the ground. The sun floated in a clear
blue sky. The sea was blue, and blue-green,
as far as the eye could see.
Scarcely a ripple. Calm. I dressed and went
for a walk – determined not to return
until I took in what Nature had to offer.
I passed close to some old, bent-over trees.
Crossed a field strewn with rocks
where snow had drifted. Kept going
until I reached the bluff.
Where I gazed at the sea, and the sky, and
the gulls wheeling over the white beach
far below. All lovely. All bathed in a pure
cold light. But, as usual, my thoughts
began to wander. I had to will
myself to see what I was seeing
and nothing else. I had to tell myself *this* is what
mattered, not the other. (And I did see it,
for a minute or two!) For a minute or two
it crowded out the usual musings on
what was right, and what was wrong – duty,
tender memories, thoughts of death, how I should treat
with my former wife. All the things
I hoped would go away this morning.
The stuff I live with every day. What
I've trampled on in order to stay alive.
But for a minute or two I did forget
myself and everything else. I know I did.
For when I turned back I didn't know

where I was. Until some birds rose up
from the gnarled trees. And flew
in the direction I needed to be going.

TWO

MEMORY

Cutting the stems from a quart
basket of strawberries – the first
this spring – looking forward to how
I would eat them tonight, when I was
alone, for a treat (Tess being away),
I remembered I forgot to pass along
a message to her when we talked:
somebody whose name I forget
called to say Susan Powell's
grandmother had died, suddenly.
Went on working with the strawberries.
But remembered, too, driving back
from the store. A little girl
on roller skates being pulled along
the road by this big friendly-
looking dog. I waved to her.
She waved back. And called out
sharply to her dog, who kept
trying to nose around
in the sweet ditch grass.
   It's nearly dark outside now.
Strawberries are chilling.
A little later on, when I eat them,
I'll be reminded again – in no particular
order – of Tess, the little girl, a dog,
roller skates, memory, death, etc.

STILL LOOKING OUT FOR
NUMBER ONE

Now that you've gone away for five days,
I'll smoke all the cigarettes I want,
where I want. Make biscuits and eat them
with jam and fat bacon. Loaf. Indulge
myself. Walk on the beach if I feel
like it. And I feel like it, alone and
thinking about when I was young. The people
then who loved me beyond reason.
And how I loved them above all others.
Except one. I'm saying I'll do everything
I want here while you're away!
But there's one thing I won't do.
I won't sleep in our bed without you.
No. It doesn't please me to do so.
I'll sleep where I damn well feel like it —
where I sleep best when you're away
and I can't hold you the way I do.
On the broken sofa in my study.

A FORGE, AND A SCYTHE

One minute I had the windows open
and the sun was out. Warm breezes
blew through the room.
(I remarked on this in a letter.)
Then, while I watched, it grew dark.
The water began whitecapping.
All the sport-fishing boats turned
and headed in, a little fleet.
Those wind–chimes on the porch
blew down. The tops of our trees shook.
The stove pipe squeaked and rattled
around in its moorings.
I said, "A forge, and a scythe."
I talk to myself like this.
Saying the names of things –
capstan, hawser, loam, leaf, furnace.
Your face, your mouth, your shoulder
inconceivable to me now!
Where did they go? It's like
I dreamed them. The stones we brought
home from the beach lie face up
on the windowsill, cooling.
Come home. Do you hear?
My lungs are thick with the smoke
of your absence.

OUR FIRST HOUSE
IN SACRAMENTO

This much is clear to me now – even then
our days were numbered. After our first week
in the house that came furnished
with somebody else's things, a man appeared
one night with a baseball bat. And raised it.
I was not the man he thought I was.
Finally, I got him to believe it.
He wept from frustration after his anger
left him. None of this had anything to do
with Beatlemania. The next week these friends
of ours from the bar where we all drank
brought friends of theirs to our house –
and we played poker. I lost the grocery money
to a stranger. Who went on to quarrel
with his wife. In his frustration
he drove his fist through the kitchen wall.
Then he, too, disappeared from my life forever.
When we left that house where nothing worked
any longer, we left at midnight
with a U-Haul trailer and a lantern.
Who knows what passed through the neighbors' minds
when they saw a family leaving their house
in the middle of the night?
The lantern moving behind the curtainless
windows. The shadows going from room to room,
gathering their things into boxes.
I saw firsthand
what frustration can do to a man.
Make him weep, make him throw his fist
through a wall. Set him to dreaming

of the house that's his
at the end of the long road. A house
filled with music, ease, and generosity.
A house that hasn't been lived in yet.

THE CAR

The car with a cracked windshield.
The car that threw a rod.
The car without brakes.
The car with a faulty U-joint.
The car with a hole in its radiator.
The car I picked peaches for.
The car with a cracked block.
The car with no reverse gear.
The car I traded for a bicycle.
The car with steering problems.
The car with no back seat.
The car with the torn front seat.
The car that burned oil.
The car with rotten hoses.
The car that left the restaurant without paying.
The car with bald tires.
The car with no heater or defroster.
The car with its front end out of alignment.
The car the child threw up in.
The car *I* threw up in.
The car with the broken water pump.
The car whose timing gear was shot.
The car with a blown head-gasket.
The car I left on the side of the road.
The car that leaked carbon monoxide.
The car with a sticky carburetor.
The car that hit the dog and kept going.
The car with a hole in its muffler.
The car with no muffler.

The car my daughter wrecked.
The car with the twice-rebuilt engine.
The car with the corroded battery cables.
The car bought with a bad check.
Car of my sleepless nights.
The car with a stuck thermostat.
The car whose engine caught fire.
The car with no headlights.
The car with a broken fan belt.
The car with wipers that wouldn't work.
The car I gave away.
The car with transmission trouble.
The car I washed my hands of.
The car I struck with a hammer.
The car with payments that couldn't be met.
The repossessed car.
The car whose clutch-pin broke.
The car waiting on the back lot.
The car of my dreams.
My car.

NYQUIL

Call it iron discipline. But for months
I never took my first drink
before eleven P.M. Not so bad,
considering. This was in the beginning
phase of things. I knew a man
whose drink of choice was Listerine.
He was coming down off Scotch.
He bought Listerine by the case,
and drank it by the case. The back seat
of his car was piled high with dead soldiers.
Those empty bottles of Listerine
gleaming in his scalding back seat!
The sight of it sent me home soul-searching.
I did that once or twice. Everybody does.
Go way down inside and look around.
I spent hours there, but
didn't meet anyone, or see anything
of interest. I came back to the here and now,
and put on my slippers. Fixed
myself a nice glass of NyQuil.
Dragged a chair over to the window.
Where I watched a pale moon struggle to rise
over Cupertino, California.
I waited through hours of darkness with NyQuil.
And then, sweet Jesus! the first sliver
of light.

LATE NIGHT WITH
FOG AND HORSES

They were in the living room. Saying their
goodbyes. Loss ringing in their ears.
They'd been through a lot together, but now
they couldn't go another step. Besides, for him
there was someone else. Tears were falling
when a horse stepped out of the fog
into the front yard. Then another, and
another. She went outside and said,
"Where did you come from, you sweet horses?"
and moved in amongst them, weeping,
touching their flanks. The horses began
to graze in the front yard.
He made two calls: one call went straight
to the sheriff – "someone's horses are out."
But there was that other call, too.
Then he joined his wife in the front
yard, where they talked and murmured
to the horses together. (Whatever was
happening now was happening in another time.)
Horses cropped the grass in the yard
that night. A red emergency light
flashed as a sedan crept in out of fog.
Voices carried out of the fog.
At the end of that long night,
when they finally put their arms around
each other, their embrace was full of
passion and memory. Each recalled
the other's youth. Now something had ended,
something else rushing in to take its place.
Came the moment of leave-taking itself.

"Goodbye, go on," she said.
And the pulling away.
Much later,
he remembered making a disastrous phone call.
One that had hung on and hung on,
a malediction. It's boiled down
to that. The rest of his life.
Malediction.

WHAT I CAN DO

All I want today is to keep an eye on these birds
outside my window. The phone is unplugged
so my loved ones can't reach out and put the arm
on me. I've told them the well has run dry.
They won't hear of it. They keep trying
to get through anyway. Just now I can't bear to know
about the car that blew another gasket.
Or the trailer I thought I'd paid for long ago,
now foreclosed on. Or the son in Italy
who threatens to end his life there
unless I keep paying the bills. My mother wants
to talk to me too. Wants to remind me again how it was
back then. All the milk I drank, cradled in her arms.
That ought to be worth something now. She needs
me to pay for this new move of hers. She'd like
to loop back to Sacramento for the twentieth time.
Everybody's luck has gone south. All I ask
is to be allowed to sit for a moment longer.
Nursing a bite the shelty dog Keeper gave me last night.
And watching these birds. Who don't ask for a thing
except sunny weather. In a minute
I'll have to plug in the phone and try to separate
what's right from wrong. Until then
a dozen tiny birds, no bigger than teacups,
perch in the branches outside the window.
Suddenly they stop singing and turn their heads.
It's clear they've felt something.
They dive into flight.

ENERGY

Last night at my daughter's, near Blaine,
she did her best to tell me
what went wrong
between her mother and me.
"Energy. You two's energy was all wrong."
She looks like her mother
when her mother was young.
Laughs like her.
Moves the drift of hair
from her forehead, like her mother.
Can take a cigarette down
to the filter in three draws,
just like her mother. I thought
this visit would be easy. Wrong.
This is hard, brother. Those years
spilling over into my sleep when I try
to sleep. To wake to find a thousand
cigarettes in the ashtray and every
light in the house burning. I can't
pretend to understand anything:
today I'll be carried
three thousand miles away into
the loving arms of another woman, not
her mother. No. She's caught
in the flywheel of a new love.
I turn off the last light
and close the door.
Moving toward whatever ancient thing
it is that works the chains
and pulls us so relentlessly on.

THE AUTHOR OF HER MISFORTUNE

For the world is the world.
And it writes no histories
that end in love.
                                      Stephen Spender

I'm not the man she claims. But
this much is true: the past is
distant, a receding coastline,
and we're all in the same boat,
a scrim of rain over the sea-lanes.
Still, I wish she wouldn't keep on
saying those things about me!
Over the long course
everything but hope lets you go, then
even that loosens its grip.
There isn't enough of anything
as long as we live. But at intervals
a sweetness appears and, given a chance,
prevails. It's true I'm happy now.
And it'd be nice if she
could hold her tongue. Stop
hating me for being happy.
Blaming me for her life. I'm afraid
I'm mixed up in her mind
with someone else. A young man
of no character, living on dreams,
who swore he'd love her forever.
One who gave her a ring, and a bracelet.
Who said, *Come with me. You can trust me.*
Things to that effect. I'm not that man.
She has me confused, as I said,
with someone else.

51

THE LITTLE ROOM

There was a great reckoning.
Words flew like stones through windows.
She yelled and yelled, like the Angel of Judgment.

Then the sun shot up, and a contrail
appeared in the morning sky.
In the sudden silence, the little room
became oddly lonely as he dried her tears.
Became like all the other little rooms on earth
light finds hard to penetrate.

Rooms where people yell and hurt each other.
And afterwards feel pain, and loneliness.
Uncertainty. The need to comfort.

ALL HER LIFE

I lay down for a nap. But every time I closed my eyes,
mares' tails passed slowly over the Strait
toward Canada. And the waves. They rolled up on the beach
and then back again. You know I don't dream.
But last night I dreamed we were watching
a burial at sea. At first I was astonished.
And then filled with regret. But you
touched my arm and said, "No, it's all right.
She was very old, and he'd loved her all her life."

NEXT YEAR

That first week in Santa Barbara wasn't the worst thing
to happen. The second week he fell on his head
while drinking, just before he had to lecture.
In the lounge, that second week, she took the microphone
from the singer's hands and crooned her own
torch song. Then danced. And then passed out
on the table. That's not the worst, either. They
went to jail that second week. He wasn't driving
so they booked him, dressed him in pajamas
and stuck him in Detox. Told him to get some sleep.
Told him he could see about his wife in the morning.
But how could he sleep when they wouldn't let him
close the door to his room?
The corridor's green light entered,
and the sound of a man weeping.
His wife had been called upon to give the alphabet
beside the road, in the middle of the night.
This is strange enough. But the cops had her
stand on one leg, close her eyes,
and try to touch her nose with her index finger.
All of which she failed to do.
She went to jail for resisting arrest.
He bailed her out when he got out of Detox.
They drove home in ruins.
This is not the worst. Their daughter had picked that night
to run away from home. She left a note:
"You're both crazy. Give me a break, PLEASE.
Don't come after me."
That's still not the worst. They went on
thinking they were the people they said they were.

Answering to those names.
Making love to the people with those names.
Nights without beginning that had no end.
Talking about a past as if it'd really happened.
Telling themselves that this time next year,
this time next year
things were going to be different.

TO MY DAUGHTER

Everything I see will outlive me.
Anna Akhmatova

It's too late now to put a curse on you – wish you
plain, say, as Yeats did his daughter. And when
we met her in Sligo, selling her paintings, it'd worked –
she *was* the plainest, oldest woman in Ireland.
But she was safe.
For the longest time, his reasoning
escaped me. Anyway, it's too late for you,
as I said. You're grownup now, and lovely.
You're a beautiful drunk, daughter.
But you're a drunk. I can't say you're breaking
my heart. I don't have a heart when it comes
to this booze thing. Sad, yes, Christ alone knows.
Your old man, the one they call Shiloh, is back
in town, and the drink has started to flow again.
You've been drunk for three days, you tell me,
when you know goddamn well drinking is like poison
to our family. Didn't your mother and I set you
example enough? Two people
who loved each other knocking each other around,
knocking back the love we felt, glass by empty glass,
curses and blows and betrayals?
You must be crazy! Wasn't all that enough for you?
You want to die? Maybe that's it. Maybe
I think I know you, and I don't.
I'm not kidding, kiddo. Who are you kidding?
Daughter, you can't drink.
The last few times I saw you, you were out of it.

A cast on your collarbone, or else
a splint on your finger, dark glasses to hide
your beautiful bruised eyes. A lip
that a man should kiss instead of split.
Oh, Jesus, Jesus, Jesus Christ!
You've got to take hold now.
Do you hear me? Wake up! You've got to knock it off
and get straight. Clean up your act. I'm asking you.
Okay, telling you. Sure, our family was made
to squander, not collect. But turn this around now.
You simply must – that's all!
Daughter, you can't drink.
It will kill you. Like it did your mother, and me.
Like it did.

FROM THE EAST, LIGHT

The house rocked and shouted all night.
Toward morning, grew quiet. The children,
looking for something to eat, make
their way through the crazy living room
in order to get to the crazy kitchen.
There's Father, asleep on the couch.
Sure they stop to look. Who wouldn't?
They listen to his violent snores
and understand that the old way of life
has begun once more. So what else is new?
But the real shocker, what makes them stare,
is that their Christmas tree has been turned over.
It lies on its side in front of the fireplace.
The tree they helped decorate.
It's wrecked now, icicles and candy canes
litter the rug. How'd a thing like this happen, anyway?
And they see Father has opened
his present from Mother. It's a length of rope
half-in, half-out of its pretty box.
Let them both go hang
themselves, is what they'd like to say.
To hell with it, and
them, is what they're thinking. Meanwhile,
there's cereal in the cupboard, milk
in the fridge. They take their bowls
in where the TV is, find their show,
try to forget about the mess everywhere.
Up goes the volume. Louder, and then louder.
Father turns over and groans. The children laugh.
They turn it up some more so he'll for sure know
he's alive. He raises his head. Morning begins.

MOTHER

My mother calls to wish me a Merry Christmas.
And to tell me if this snow keeps on
she intends to kill herself. I want to say
I'm not myself this morning, please
give me a break. I may have to borrow a psychiatrist
again. The one who always asks me the most fertile
of questions, "But what are you *really* feeling?"
Instead, I tell her one of our skylights
has a leak. While I'm talking, the snow is
melting onto the couch. I say I've switched to All-Bran
so there's no need to worry any longer
about me getting cancer, and her money coming to an end.
She hears me out. Then informs me
she's leaving *this goddamn place*. Somehow. The only time
she wants to see it, or me again, is from her coffin.
Suddenly, I ask if she remembers the time Dad
was dead drunk and bobbed the tail of the Labrador pup.
I go on like this for a while, talking about
those days. She listens, waiting her turn.
It continues to snow. It snows and snows
as I hang on the phone. The trees and rooftops
are covered with it. How can I talk about this?
How can I possibly explain what I'm feeling?

UNION STREET: SAN FRANCISCO, SUMMER 1975

In those days we were going places. But that Sunday
afternoon we were becalmed. Sitting around a table,
drinking and swapping stories. A party that'd been
going on, and off, since Friday a year ago.
Then Guy's wife was dropped off in front of the apartment
by her boyfriend, and came upstairs.
It's Guy's birthday, after all, give or take a day.
They haven't seen each other for a week,
more or less. She's all dressed up. He embraces her,
sort of, makes her a drink. Finds a place
for her at the table. Everyone wants to know
how she is, etc. But she ignores them all.
All those alcoholics. Clearly, she's pissed off
and as usual in the wrong company.
Where the hell has Guy been keeping himself?
she wants to know. She sips her drink and looks at him
as if he's brain-damaged. She spots a pimple
on his chin; it's an ingrown hair but it's filled
with pus, frightful, looks like hell. In front
of everyone she says, "Who have *you* been eating out
lately?" Staring hard at his pimple.
Being drunk myself, I don't recall how he answered.
Maybe he said, "I don't remember who it was;
I didn't get her name." Something smart.
Anyway, his wife has this kind of blistery rash,
maybe it's cold sores, at the edge of her mouth,
so she shouldn't be talking. Pretty soon,

it's like always: they're holding hands and laughing
like the rest of us, at little or nothing.

                    Later, in the living room,
thinking everyone had gone out for hamburgers,
she blew him in front of the TV. Then said,
"Happy birthday, you son of a bitch!" And slapped his
glasses off. The glasses he'd been wearing
while she made love to him. I walked into the room
and said, "Friends, don't do this to each other."
She didn't flinch a muscle or wonder aloud
which rock I'd come out from under. All she said was
"Who asked you, hobo-urine?" Guy put his glasses on.
Pulled his trousers up. We all went out
to the kitchen and had a drink. Then another. Like that,
the world had gone from afternoon to night.

ROMANTICISM

*(for Linda Gregg,
after reading "Classicism")*

The nights are very unclear here.
But if the moon is full, we know it.
We feel one thing one minute,
something else the next.

ANATHEMA

The entire household suffered.
My wife, myself, the two children, and the dog
whose puppies were born dead.
Our affairs, such as they were, withered.
My wife was dropped by her lover,
the one-armed teacher of music who was
her only contact with the outside world
and the things of the mind.
My own girlfriend said she couldn't stand it
anymore, and went back to her husband.
The water was shut off.
All that summer the house baked.
The peach trees were blasted.
Our little flower bed lay trampled.
The brakes went out on the car, and the battery
failed. The neighbors quit speaking
to us and closed their doors in our faces.
Checks flew back at us from merchants –
and then mail stopped being delivered
altogether. Only the sheriff got through
from time to time – with one or the other
of our children in the back seat,
pleading to be taken anywhere but here.
And then mice entered the house in droves.
Followed by a bull snake. My wife
found it sunning itself in the living room
next to the dead TV. How she dealt with it
is another matter. Chopped its head off
right there on the floor.

And then chopped it in two when it continued
to writhe. We saw we couldn't hold out
any longer. We were beaten.
We wanted to get down on our knees
and say forgive us our sins, forgive us
our lives. But it was too late.
Too late. No one would listen.
We had to watch as the house was pulled down,
the ground plowed up, and then
we were dispersed in four directions.

THE AUTOPSY ROOM

Then I was young and had the strength of ten.
For anything, I thought. Though part of my job
at night was to clean the autopsy room
once the coroner's work was done. But now
and then they knocked off early, or too late.
For, so help me, they left things out
on their specially built table. A little baby,
still as a stone and snow cold. Another time,
a huge black man with white hair whose chest
had been laid open. All his vital organs
lay in a pan beside his head. The hose
was running, the overhead lights blazed.
And one time there was a leg, a woman's leg,
on the table. A pale and shapely leg.
I knew it for what it was. I'd seen them before.
Still, it took my breath away..

When I went home at night my wife would say,
"Sugar, it's going to be all right. We'll trade
this life in for another." But it wasn't
that easy. She'd take my hand between her hands
and hold it tight, while I leaned back on the sofa
and closed my eyes. Thinking of . . . something.
I don't know what. But I'd let her bring
my hand to her breast. At which point
I'd open my eyes and stare at the ceiling, or else
the floor. Then my fingers strayed to her leg.
Which was warm and shapely, ready to tremble
and raise slightly, at the slightest touch.

But my mind was unclear and shaky. Nothing
was happening. Everything was happening. Life
was a stone, grinding and sharpening.

HOPE

"My wife," said Pinnegar, *"expects to see me go the dogs*
when she leaves me. It is her last hope."
D. H. Lawrence,
"Jimmy and the Desperate Woman"

She gave me the car and two
hundred dollars. Said, So long, baby.
Take it easy, hear? So much
for twenty years of marriage.
She knows, or thinks she knows,
I'll go through the dough
in a day or two, and eventually
wreck the car – which was
in my name and needed work anyway.
When I drove off, she and her boyfriend were changing the lock
on the front door. They waved.
I waved back to let them know
I didn't think any the less
of them. Then sped toward
the state line. I *was* hell-bent.
She was right to think so.

I went to the dogs, and we
became good friends.
But I kept going. Went
a long way without stopping.
Left the dogs, my friends, behind.
Nevertheless, when I did show
my face at that house again,
months, or years, later, driving
a different car, she wept

67

when she saw me at the door.
Sober. Dressed in a clean shirt,
pants, and boots. Her last hope
blasted.
She didn't have a thing
to hope for anymore.

WHERE THEY'D LIVED

Everywhere he went that day he walked
in his own past. Kicked through piles
of memories. Looked through windows
that no longer belonged to him.
Work and poverty and short change.
In those days they'd lived by their wills,
determined to be invincible.
Nothing could stop them. Not
for the longest while.

                In the motel room
that night, in the early morning hours,
he opened a curtain. Saw clouds
banked against the moon. He leaned
closer to the glass. Cold air passed
through and put its hand over his heart.
I loved you, he thought.
Loved you well.
Before loving you no longer.

JEAN'S TV

My life's on an even keel
these days. Though who's to say
it'll never waver again?
This morning I recalled
a girlfriend I had just after
my marriage broke up.
A sweet girl named Jean.
In the beginning, she had no idea
how bad things were. It took
a while. But she loved me
a bunch anyway, she said.

And I know that's true.
She let me stay at her place
where I conducted
the shabby business of my life
over her phone. She bought
my booze, but told me
I wasn't a drunk
like those others said.
Signed checks for me
and left them on her pillow
when she went off to work.
Gave me a Pendleton jacket
that Christmas, one I still wear.

For my part, I taught her to drink.
And how to fall asleep
with her clothes on.
How to wake up

weeping in the middle of the night.
When I left, she paid two months'
rent for me. And gave me
her black and white TV.

We talked on the phone once,
months later. She was drunk.
And, sure, I was drunk too.
The last thing she said to me was
Will I ever see my TV again?
I looked around the room
as if the TV might suddenly
appear in its place
on the kitchen chair. Or else
come out of a cupboard
and declare itself. But that TV
had gone down the road
weeks before. The TV Jean gave me.

I didn't tell her that.
I lied, of course. Soon, I said,
very soon now.
And put down the phone
after, or before, she hung up.
But those sleep-sounding words
of mine making me feel
I'd come to the end of a story.
And now, this one last falsehood
behind me,
                    I could rest.

TOMORROW

Cigarette smoke hanging on
in the living room. The ship's lights
out on the water, dimming. The stars
burning holes in the sky. Becoming ash, yes.
But it's all right, they're supposed to do that.
Those lights we call stars.
Burn for a time and then die.
Me hell–bent. Wishing
it were tomorrow already.
I remember my mother, God love her,
saying, Don't wish for tomorrow.
You're wishing your life away.
Nevertheless, I wish
for tomorrow. In all its finery.
I want sleep to come and go, smoothly.
Like passing out of the door of one car
into another. And then to wake up!
Find tomorrow in my bedroom.
I'm more tired now than I can say.
My bowl is empty. But it's my bowl, you see,
and I love it.

THE TRESTLE

I've wasted my time this morning, and I'm deeply ashamed.
I went to bed last night thinking about my dad.
About that little river we used to fish – Butte Creek –
near Lake Almanor. Water lulled me to sleep.
In my dream, it was all I could do not to get up
and move around. But when I woke early this morning
I went to the telephone instead. Even though
the river was flowing down there in the valley,
in the meadows, moving through ditch clover.
Fir trees stood on both sides of the meadows. And I was there.
A kid sitting on a timber trestle, looking down.
Watching my dad drink from his cupped hands.
Then he said, "This water's so good.
I wish I could give my mother some of this water."
My dad still loved her, though she was dead
and he'd been away from her for a long time.
He had to wait some more years
until he could go where she was. But he loved
this country where he found himself. The West.
For thirty years it had him around the heart,
and then it let him go. He went to sleep one night
in a town in northern California
and didn't wake up. What could be simpler?

I wish my own life, and death, could be so simple.
So that when I woke on a fine morning like this,
after being somewhere I wanted to be all night,
somewhere important, I could move most naturally
and without thinking about it, to my desk.

Say I did that, in the simple way I've described.
From bed to desk back to childhood.
From there it's not so far to the trestle.
And from the trestle I could look down
and see my dad when I needed to see him.
My dad drinking that cold water. My sweet father.
The river, its meadows, and firs, and the trestle.
That. Where I once stood.

I wish I could do that
without having to plead with myself for it.
And feel sick of myself
for getting involved in lesser things.
I know it's time I changed my life.
This life – the one with its complications
and phone calls – is unbecoming,
and a waste of time.
I want to plunge my hands in clear water. The way
he did. Again and then again.

HARLEY'S SWANS

I'm trying again. A man has to begin
over and over — to try to think and feel
only in a very limited field, the house
on the street, the man at the corner drug store.
  Sherwood Anderson, *from a letter*

Anderson, I thought of you when I loitered
in front of the drug store this afternoon.
Held onto my hat in the wind and looked down
the street for my boyhood. Remembered my dad
taking me to get haircuts —

that rack of antlers mounted on a wall
next to the calendar picture of a rainbow
trout leaping clear of the water
with a hook in its jaw. My mother.
How she went with me to pick out
school clothes. That part embarrassing
because I needed to shop in men's wear
for man-sized pants and shirts.
Nobody, then, who could love me,
the fattest kid on the block, except my parents.

So I quit looking and went inside.
Had a Coke at the soda fountain
where I gave some thought to betrayal.
How that part always came easy.
It was what came after that was hard.
I didn't think about you anymore, Anderson.
You'd come and gone in an instant.
But I remembered, there at the fountain,
Harley's swans. How they got there

I don't know. But one morning he was taking
his school bus along a country road
when he came across 21 of them just down
from Canada. Out on this pond
in a farmer's field. He brought his school bus
to a stop, and then he and his grade-schoolers
just looked at them for a while and felt good.

I finished the Coke and drove home.
It was almost dark now. The house
quiet and empty. The way
I always thought I wanted it to be.
The wind blew hard all day.
Blew everything away, or nearly.
But still this feeling of shame and loss.
Even though the wind ought to lay now
and the moon come out soon, if this is
anything like the other nights.
I'm here in the house. And I want to try again.
You, of all people, Anderson, can understand.

THE CRANES

Cranes lifting up out of the marshland . . .
My brother brings his fingers to his temples
and then drops his hands.

Like that, he was dead.
The satin lining of autumn.
O my brother! I miss you now, and I'd like to have you back.

Hug you like a grown man
who knows the worth of things.
The mist of events drifts away.

Not in this life, I told you once.
I was given a different set of marching orders.
I planned to go mule-backing across the Isthmus.

Begone, though, if this is your idea of things!
But I'll think of you out there
when I look at those stars we saw as children.

The cranes wallop their wings.
In a moment, they'll find true north.
Then turn in the opposite direction.

THREE

FOR TESS

Out on the Strait the water is whitecapping,
as they say here. It's rough, and I'm glad
I'm not out. Glad I fished all day
on Morse Creek, casting a red Daredevil back
and forth. I didn't catch anything. No bites
even, not one. But it was okay. It was fine!
I carried your dad's pocketknife and was followed
for a while by a dog its owner called Dixie.
At times I felt so happy I had to quit
fishing. Once I lay on the bank with my eyes closed,
listening to the sound the water made,
and to the wind in the tops of the trees. The same wind
that blows out on the Strait, but a different wind, too.
For a while I even let myself imagine I had died —
and that was all right, at least for a couple
of minutes, until it really sank in: *Dead*.
As I was lying there with my eyes closed,
just after I'd imagined what it might be like
if in fact I never got up again, I thought of you.
I opened my eyes then and got right up
and went back to being happy again.
I'm grateful to you, you see. I wanted to tell you.

A HAIRCUT

So many impossible things have already
happened in this life. He doesn't think
twice when she tells him to get ready:
He's about to get a haircut.

He sits in the chair in the upstairs room,
the room they sometimes joke and refer to
as the library. There's a window there
that gives light. Snow's coming
down outside as newspapers go down
around his feet. She drapes a big
towel over his shoulders. Then
gets out her scissors, comb, and brush.

This is the first time they've been
alone together in a while – with nobody
going anywhere, or needing to do
anything. Not counting the going
to bed with each other. That intimacy.
Or breakfasting together. Another
intimacy. They both grow quiet
and thoughtful as she cuts his hair,
and combs it, and cuts some more.
The snow keeps falling outside.
Soon, light begins to pull away
from the window. He stares down, lost and
musing, trying to read
something from the paper. She says,
"Raise your head." And he does.

And then she says, "See what you think
of it." He goes to look
in the mirror, and it's fine.
It's just the way he likes it,
and he tells her so.

It's later, when he turns on the
porchlight, and shakes out the towel
and sees the curls and swaths of
white and dark hair fly out onto
the snow and stay there,
that he understands something: He's
grownup now, a real, grownup,
middle-aged man. When he was a boy,
going with his dad to the barbershop,
or even later, a teenager, how
could he have imagined his life
would someday allow him the privilege of
a beautiful woman to travel with,
and sleep with, and take his breakfast with?
Not only that — a woman who would
quietly cut his hair in the afternoon
in a dark city that lay under snow
3000 miles away from where he'd started.
A woman who could look at him
across the table and say,
"It's time to put you in the barber's
chair. It's time somebody gave you
a haircut."

HAPPINESS IN CORNWALL

His wife died, and he grew old
between the graveyard and his
front door. Walked with a gait.
Shoulders bent. He let his clothes
go, and his long hair turned white.
His children found him somebody.
A big middle-aged woman with
heavy shoes who knew how to
mop, wax, dust, shop, and carry in
firewood. Who could live
in a room at the back of the house.
Prepare meals. And slowly,
slowly bring the old man around
to listening to her read poetry
in the evenings in front of
the fire. Tennyson, Browning,
Shakespeare, Drinkwater. Men
whose names take up space
on the page. She was the butler,
cook, housekeeper. And after
a time, oh, no one knows or cares
when, they began to dress up
on Sundays and stroll through town.
She with her arm through his.
Smiling. He proud and happy
and with his hand on hers.
No one denied them
or tried to diminish this
in any way. Happiness is
a rare thing! Evenings he

listened to poetry, poetry, poetry
in front of the fire.
Couldn't get enough of that life.

VENICE

The gondolier handed you a rose.
Took us up one canal
and then another. We glided
past Casanova's palace, the palace of
the Rossi family, palaces belonging
to the Baglioni, the Pisani, and Sangallo.
Flooded. Stinking. What's left
left to rats. Blackness.
The silence total, or nearly.
The man's breath coming and going
behind my ear. The dip of the oar.
We gliding silently on, and on.
Who would blame me if I fall
to thinking about death?
A shutter opened above our heads.
A little light showed through
before the shutter was closed once
more. There is that, and the rose
in your hand. And history.

THE LIGHTNING SPEED OF THE PAST

The corpse fosters anxiety in men who believe
in the Last Judgment, and those who don't.
                                        André Malraux

He buried his wife, who'd died in
misery. In misery, he
took to his porch, where he watched
the sun set and the moon rise.
The days seemed to pass, only to return
again. Like a dream in which one thinks,
I've already dreamt that.

Nothing, having arrived, will stay.
With his knife he cut the skin
from an apple. The white pulp, body
of the apple, darkened
and turned brown, then black,
before his eyes. The worn-out face of death!
The lightning speed of the past.

WENAS RIDGE

The seasons turning. Memory flaring.
Three of us that fall. Young hoodlums –
shoplifters, stealers of hubcaps.
Bozos. Dick Miller, dead now.
Lyle Rousseau, son of the Ford dealer.
And I, who'd just made a girl pregnant.
Hunting late into that golden afternoon
for grouse. Following deer paths,
pushing through undergrowth, stepping over
blow-downs. Reaching out for something to hold onto.

At the top of Wenas Ridge
we walked out of pine trees and could see
down deep ravines, where the wind roared, to the river.
More alive then, I thought, than I'd ever be.
But my whole life, in switchbacks, ahead of me.

Hawks, deer, coons we looked at and let go.
Killed six grouse and should have stopped.
Didn't, though we had limits.

Lyle and I climbing fifty feet or so
above Dick Miller. Who screamed – "Yaaaah!"
Then swore and swore. Legs numbing as I saw what.
That fat, dark snake rising up. Beginning to sing.
And how it sang! A timber rattler thick as my wrist.
It'd struck at Miller, but missed. No other way
to say it – he was paralyzed. Could scream, and swear,
not shoot. Then the snake lowered itself from sight
and went in under rocks. We understood

we'd have to get down. In the same way we'd got up.
Blindly crawling through brush, stepping over blow-downs,
pushing into undergrowth. Shadows falling from trees now
onto flat rocks that held the day's heat. And snakes.
My heart stopped, and then started again.
My hair stood on end. This was the moment
my life had prepared me for. And I wasn't ready.

We started down anyway. Jesus, please help me
out of this, I prayed. I'll believe in you again
and honor you always. But Jesus was crowded out
of my head by the vision of that rearing snake.
That singing. Keep believing in me, snake said,
for I will return. I made an obscure, criminal pact
that day. Praying to Jesus in one breath.
To snake in the other. Snake finally more real
to me. The memory of that day
like a blow to the calf now.

I got out, didn't I? But something happened.
I married the girl I loved, yet poisoned her life.
Lies began to coil in my heart and call it home.
Got used to darkness and its crooked ways.
Since then I've always feared rattlesnakes.
Been ambivalent about Jesus.
But someone, something's responsible for this.
Now, as then.

BLOOD

We were five at the craps table
not counting the croupier
and his assistant. The man
next to me had the dice
cupped in his hand.
He blew on his fingers, said
Come *on*, baby! And leaned
over the table to throw.
At that moment, bright blood rushed
from his nose, spattering
the green felt cloth. He dropped
the dice. Stepped back amazed.
And then terrified as blood
ran down his shirt. God,
what's happening to me?
he cried. Took hold of my arm.
I heard Death's engines turning.
But I was young at the time,
and drunk, and wanted to play.
I didn't have to listen.
So I walked away. Didn't turn back, ever,
or find this in my head, until today.

LIMITS

All that day, we banged at geese
from a blind at the top
of the bluff. Busted one flock
after the other, until our gun barrels
grew hot to the touch. Geese
filled the cold, gray air. But we still
didn't kill our limits.
The wind driving our shot
every whichway. Late afternoon,
and we had four. Two shy
of our limits. Thirst drove us
off the bluff and down a dirt road
alongside the river.

To an evil-looking farm
surrounded by dead fields of
barley. Where, almost evening,
a man with patches of skin
gone from his hands let us dip water
from a bucket on his porch.
Then asked if we wanted to see
something – a Canada goose he kept
alive in a barrel beside
the barn. The barrel covered over
with screen wire, rigged inside
like a little cell. He'd broken
the bird's wing with a long shot,
he said, then chased it down
and stuffed it in the barrel.
He'd had a brainstorm!

He'd use that goose as a live decoy.

In time it turned out to be
the damnedest thing he'd ever seen.
It would bring other geese
right down on your head.
So close you could almost touch them
before you killed them.
This man, he never wanted for geese.
And for this his goose was given
all the corn and barley
it could eat, and a barrel
to live in, and shit in.

I took a good long look and,
unmoving, the goose looked back.
Only its eyes telling me
it was alive. Then we left,
my friend and I. Still
willing to kill anything
that moved, anything that rose
over our sights. I don't
recall if we got anything else
that day. I doubt it.
It was almost dark anyhow.
No matter, now. But for years
and years afterwards, living
on a staple of bitterness, I
didn't forget that goose.
I set it apart from all the others,
living and dead. Came to understand
one can get used to anything,
and become a stranger to nothing.
Saw that betrayal is just another word
for loss, for hunger.

THE WHITE FIELD

Woke up feeling anxious and bone-lonely.
Unable to give my attention to anything
beyond coffee and cigarettes. Of course,
the best antidote for this is work.
"What is your duty? What each day requires,"
said Goethe, or someone like him.
But I didn't have any sense of duty.
I didn't feel like doing anything.
I felt as if I'd lost my will, and my memory.
And I had. If someone had come along
at that minute, as I was slurping coffee, and said,
"Where were you when I needed you?
How have you spent your life? What'd you do
even two days ago?" What could I have said?
I'd only have gawped. Then I tried.
Remembered back a couple of days.
Driving to the end of that road with Morris.
Taking our fishing gear from the jeep.
Strapping on snowshoes, and walking across the white field
toward the river. Every so often
turning around to look at the strange tracks
we'd left. Feeling glad enough to be alive
as we kicked up rabbits, and ducks passed over.

Then to come upon Indians standing in the river
in chest-high waders! Dragging a net for steelhead
through the pool we planned to fish.
The hole just above the river's mouth.
Them working in relentless silence. Cigarettes
hanging from their lips. Not once

looking up or otherwise acknowledging
our existence.

"Christ almighty," Morris said.
"This is for the birds." And we snowshoed back
across the field, cursing our luck, cursing Indians.
The day in all other respects unremarkable.
Except when I was driving the jeep
and Morris showed me the three-inch scar
across the back of his hand from the hot stove
he'd fallen against in elk camp.

But this happened the day before yesterday.
It's yesterday that got away, that slipped through
the net and back to sea.

Yet hearing those distant voices down the road just now,
I seem to recall everything. And I understand
that yesterday had its own relentless logic.
Just like today, and all the other days in my life.

THE WINDOW

A storm blew in last night and knocked out
the electricity. When I looked
through the window, the trees were translucent.
Bent and covered with rime. A vast calm
lay over the countryside.
I knew better. But at that moment
I felt I'd never in my life made any
false promises, nor committed
so much as one indecent act. My thoughts
were virtuous. Later on that morning,
of course, electricity was restored.
The sun moved from behind the clouds,
melting the hoarfrost.
And things stood as they had before.

ITS COURSE

The man who took 38 steelhead out
of this little river
last winter (his name is Bill Zitter,
"last name in the directory")
told me the river's changed its course
dramatically, he would even say
radically, since he first moved here,
he and his wife. It used to flow
"yonder, where those houses are."
When salmon crossed that shoal at night,
they made a noise like water boiling
in a cauldron, a noise like you were
scrubbing something on a washboard.
"It could wake you up from a deep sleep."
Now, there's no more salmon run.
And he won't fish for steelhead
this winter, because Mrs Zitter's
eaten up with cancer. He's needed
at home. The doctors expect
she'll pass away before the New Year.

"Right where you're living," he goes on,
"that used to be a motorcycle run.
They'd come from all over the county
to race their bikes. They'd tear up
that hill and then go down
the other side. But they were
just having fun. Young guys. Not
like those gangs today, those bad apples."
I wished him luck. Shook his hand.

And went home to my house, the place
they used to race motorcycles.

Later, at the table in my room, looking
out over the water, I give some thought
to just what it is I'm doing here.
What it is I'm after in this life.
It doesn't seem like much,
in the end. I remembered what he'd said
about the young men
and their motorcycles.
Those young men who must be old men
now. Zitter's age, or else
my age. Old enough, in either case.
And for a moment I imagine
the roar of the engines as they surge
up this hill, the laughter and
shouting as they spill, swear, get up,
shake themselves off, and walk
their bikes to the top.
Where they slap each other on the back
and reach in the burlap bag for a beer.
Now and then one of them gunning it
for all it's worth, forcing his way
to the top, and then going lickety-
split down the other side!
Disappearing in a roar, in a cloud of dust.
Right outside my window is where
all this happened. We vanish soon enough.
Soon enough, eaten up.

SINEW

The girl minding the store.
She stands at the window
picking a piece of pork
from her teeth. Idly
watching the men in serge suits,
waistcoats, and ties,
dapping for trout on Lough Gill,
near the Isle of Innisfree.
The remains of her midday meal
congealing on the sill.
The air is still and warm.
A cuckoo calls.

Close in, a man in a boat,
wearing a hat, looks
toward shore, the little store,
and the girl. He looks, whips
his line, and looks some more.
She leans closer to the glass.
Goes out then to the lakeside.
But it's the cuckoo in the bush
that has her attention.

The man strikes a fish,
all business now.
The girl goes on working
at the sinew in her teeth.
But she watches this well-dressed
man reaching out
to slip a net under his fish.

In a minute, shyly, he floats near.
Holds up his catch for the girl's pleasure.
Doffs his hat. She stirs and smiles
a little. Raises her hand.
A gesture which starts the bird
in flight, toward Innisfree.

The man casts and casts again.
His line cuts the air. His fly
touches the water, and waits.
But what does this man
really care for trout?
What he'll take
from this day is the memory of
a girl working her finger
inside her mouth as their glances
meet, and a bird flies up.

They look at each other and smile.
In the still afternoon.
With not a word lost between them.

EAGLES

It was a sixteen-inch ling cod that the eagle
dropped near our feet
at the top of Bagley Creek canyon,
at the edge of the green woods.
Puncture marks in the sides of the fish
where the bird gripped with its talons!
That and a piece torn out of the fish's back.
Like an old painting recalled,
or an ancient memory coming back,
that eagle flew with the fish from the Strait
of Juan de Fuca up the canyon to where
the woods begin, and we stood watching.
It lost the fish above our heads,
dropped for it, missed it, and soared on
over the valley where wind beats all day.
We watched it keep going until it was
a speck, then gone. I picked up
the fish. That miraculous ling cod.
Came home from the walk and –
why the hell not? – cooked it
lightly in oil and ate it
with boiled potatoes and peas and biscuits.
Over dinner, talking about eagles
and an older, fiercer order of things.

ELK CAMP

Everyone else sleeping when I step
to the door of our tent. Overhead,
stars brighter than stars ever were
in my life. And farther away.
The November moon driving
a few dark clouds over the valley.
The Olympic Range beyond.

I believed I could smell the snow that was coming.
Our horses feeding inside
the little rope corral we'd thrown up.
From the side of the hill the sound
of spring water. Our spring water.
Wind passing in the tops of the fir trees.
I'd never smelled a forest before that
night, either. Remembered reading how
Henry Hudson and his sailors smelled
the forests of the New World
from miles out at sea. And then the next thought –
I could gladly live the rest of my life
and never pick up another book.
I looked at my hands in the moonlight
and understood there wasn't a man,
woman, or child I could lift a finger
for that night. I turned back and lay
down then in my sleeping bag.
But my eyes wouldn't close.

The next day I found cougar scat
and elk droppings. But though I rode

a horse all over that country,
up and down hills, through clouds
and along old logging roads,
I never saw an elk. Which was
fine by me. Still, I was ready.
Lost to everyone, a rifle strapped
to my shoulder. I think maybe
I could have killed one.
Would have shot at one, anyway.
Aimed just where I'd been told –
behind the shoulder at the heart
and lungs. "They might run,
but they won't run far.
Look at it this way," my friend said.
"How far would you run with a piece
of lead in your heart?" That depends,
my friend. That depends. But that day
I could have pulled the trigger
on anything. Or not.
Nothing mattered anymore
except getting back to camp
before dark. Wonderful
to live this way! Where nothing
mattered more than anything else.
I saw myself through and through.
And I understood something, too,
as my life flew back to me there in the woods.

And then we packed out. Where the first
thing I did was take a hot bath.
And then reach for this book.
Grow cold and unrelenting once more.
Heartless. Every nerve alert.
Ready to kill, or not.

EARWIGS

for Mona Simpson

Your delicious-looking rum cake, covered with
almonds, was hand-carried to my door
this morning. The driver parked at the foot
of the hill, and climbed the steep path.
Nothing else moved in that frozen landscape.
It was cold inside and out. I signed
for it, thanked him, went back in.
Where I stripped off the heavy tape, tore
the staples from the bag, and inside
found the canister you'd filled with cake.
I scratched adhesive from the lid.
Prized it open. Folded back the aluminum foil.
To catch the first whiff of that sweetness!

It was then the earwig appeared
from the moist depths. An earwig
stuffed on your cake. Drunk
from it. He went over the side of the can.
Scurried wildly across the table to take
refuge in the fruit bowl. I didn't kill it.
Not then. Filled as I was with conflicting
feelings. Disgust, of course. But
amazement. Even admiration. This creature
that'd just made a 3000-mile, overnight trip
by air, surrounded by cake, shaved almonds,
and the overpowering odor of rum. Carried
then in a truck over a mountain road and
packed uphill in freezing weather to a house
overlooking the Pacific Ocean. An earwig.
I'll let him live, I thought. What's one more,

or less, in the world? This one's special,
maybe. Blessings on its strange head.

I lifted the cake from its foil wrapping
and three more earwigs went over the side
of the can! For a minute I was so taken
aback I didn't know if I should kill them,
or what. Then rage seized me, and
I plastered them. Crushed the life from them
before any could get away. It was a massacre.
While I was at it, I found and destroyed
the other one utterly.
I was just beginning when it was all over.
I'm saying I could have gone on and on,
rending them. If it's true
that man is wolf to man, what can mere earwigs
expect when bloodlust is up?

I sat down, trying to quieten my heart.
Breath rushing from my nose. I looked
around the table, slowly. Ready
for anything. Mona, I'm sorry to say this,
but I couldn't eat any of your cake.
I've put it away for later, maybe.
Anyway, thanks. You're sweet to remember
me out here alone this winter.
Living alone.
Like an animal, I think.

THE FISHING POLE OF
THE DROWNED MAN

I didn't want to use it at first.
Then I thought, no, it would
give up secrets and bring me luck –
that's what I needed then.
Besides, he'd left it behind for me
to use when he went swimming that time.
Shortly afterwards, I met two women.
One of them loved opera and the other
was a drunk who'd done time
in jail. I took up with one
and began to drink and fight a lot.
The way this woman could sing and carry on!
We went straight to the bottom.

MY BOAT

My boat is being made to order. Right now it's about to leave
the hands of its builders. I've reserved a special place
for it down at the marina. It's going to have plenty of room
on it for all my friends: Richard, Bill, Chuck, Toby, Jim, Hayden,
Gary, George, Harold, Don, Dick, Scott, Geoffrey, Jack,
Paul, Jay, Morris, and Alfredo. All my friends! They know who
    they are.
Tess, of course. I wouldn't go anyplace without her.
And Kristina, Merry, Catherine, Diane, Sally, Annick, Pat,
    Judith, Susie, Lynne, Cindy, Jean, Mona.
Doug and Amy! They're family, but they're also my friends,
and they like a good time. There's room on my boat
for just about everyone. I'm serious about this!
There'll be a place on board for everyone's stories.
My own, but also the ones belonging to my friends.
Short stories, and the ones that go on and on. The true
and the made-up. The ones already finished, and the ones still
    being written.
Poems, too! Lyric poems, and the longer, darker narratives.
For my painter friends, paints and canvases will be on board
    my boat.
We'll have fried chicken, lunch meats, cheeses, rolls,
French bread. Every good thing that my friends and I like.
And a big basket of fruit, in case anyone wants fruit.
In case anyone wants to say he or she ate an apple,
or some grapes, on my boat. Whatever my friends want,
name it, and it'll be there. Soda pop of all kinds.
Beer and wine, sure. No one will be denied anything, on
    my boat.
We'll go out into the sunny harbor and have fun, that's the idea.

Just have a good time all around. Not thinking
about this or that or getting ahead or falling behind.
Fishing poles if anyone wants to fish. The fish are out there!
We may even go a little way down the coast, on my boat.
But nothing dangerous, nothing too serious.
The idea is simply to enjoy ourselves and not get scared.
We'll eat and drink and laugh a lot, on my boat.
I've always wanted to take at least one trip like this,
with my friends, on my boat. If we want to
we'll listen to Schumann on the CBC.
But if that doesn't work out, okay,
we'll switch to KRAB, The Who, and the Rolling Stones.
Whatever makes my friends happy! Maybe everyone
will have their own radio, on my boat. In any case,
we're going to have a big time. People are going to have fun,
and do what they want to do, on my boat.

SHOOTING

I wade through wheat up to my belly,
cradling a shotgun in my arms.
Tess is asleep back at the ranch house.
The moon pales. Then loses face completely
as the sun spears up over the mountains.

Why do I pick this moment
to remember my aunt taking me aside that time
and saying, *What I am going to tell you now
you will remember every day of your life?*
But that's all I can remember.

I've never been able to trust memory. My own
or anyone else's. I'd like to know what on earth
I'm doing here in this strange regalia.
It's my friend's wheat – this much is true.
And right now, his dog is on point.

Tess is opposed to killing for sport,
or any other reason. Yet not long ago she
threatened to kill me. The dog inches forward.
I stop moving. I can't see or hear
my breath any longer.

Step by tiny step, the day advances. Suddenly,
the air explodes with birds.
Tess sleeps through it. When she wakes,
October will be over. Guns and talk
of shooting behind us.

CUTLERY

Trolling the coho fly twenty feet behind the boat,
under moonlight, when the huge salmon hit it!
And lunged clear of the water. Stood, it seemed,
on its tail. Then fell back and was gone.
Shaken, I steered on into the harbor as if
nothing had happened. But it had.
And it happened in just the way I've said.
I took the memory with me to New York,
and beyond. Took it wherever I went.
All the way down here onto the terrace
of the Jockey Club in Rosario, Argentina.
Where I look out onto the broad river
that throws back light from the open windows
of the dining room. I stand smoking a cigar,
listening to the murmuring of the officers
and their wives inside; the little clashing
sound of cutlery against plates. I'm alive
and well, neither happy nor unhappy,
here in the Southern Hemisphere. So I'm all the more
astonished when I recall that lost fish rising,
leaving the water, and then returning.
The feeling of loss that gripped me then
grips me still. How can I communicate what I feel
about any of this? Inside, they go on
conversing in their own language.
                            I decide to walk
alongside the river. It's the kind of night
that brings men and rivers close.
I go for a ways, then stop. Realizing

that I haven't been close. Not
in the longest time. There's been
this waiting that's gone along with me
wherever I go. But the hope widening now
that something will rise up and splash.
I want to hear it, and move on.

FOUR

WORK

for John Gardner, d. September 14, 1982

Love of work. The blood singing
in that. The fine high rise
of it into the work. A man says,
I'm working. Or, I worked today.
Or, I'm trying to make it work.
Him working seven days a week.
And being awakened in the morning
by his young wife, his head on the typewriter.
The fullness before work.
The amazed understanding after.
Fastening his helmet.
Climbing onto his motorcycle
and thinking about home.
And work. Yes, work. The going
to what lasts.

CADILLACS AND POETRY

New snow onto old ice last night. Now,
errand-bound to town, preoccupied with the mudge
in his head, he applied his brakes too fast.
And found himself in a big car out of control,
moving broadside down the road in the immense
stillness of the winter morning. Headed
inexorably for the intersection.
The things that were passing through his mind?
The news film on TV of three alley cats
and a rhesus monkey with electrodes implanted
in their skulls; the time he stopped to photograph
a buffalo near where the Little Big Horn
joined the Big Horn; his new graphite rod
with the Limited Lifetime Warranty;
the polyps the doctor'd found on his bowel;
the Bukowski line that flew
through his mind from time to time:
We'd all like to pass by in a 1995 Cadillac.
His head a hive of arcane activity.
Even during the time it took his car
to slide around on the highway and point him
back in the direction he'd come from.
The direction of home, and relative security.
The engine was dead. The immense stillness
descended once more. He took off his woolen cap
and wiped his forehead. But after a moment's
consideration, started his car, turned around
and continued on into town.
More carefully, yes. But thinking all the while
along the same lines as before. Old ice, new snow.

Cats. A monkey. Fishing. Wild buffalo.
The sheer poetry in musing on Cadillacs
that haven't been built yet. The chastening effect
of the doctor's fingers.

THE HAT

Walking around on our first day
in Mexico City, we come to a sidewalk café
on Reforma Avenue where a man in a hat
sits drinking a beer.
At first the man seems just like any
other man, wearing a hat, drinking a beer
in the middle of the day. But next to this man,
asleep on the broad sidewalk, is a bear
with its head on its paws. The bear's
eyes are closed, but not all the way. As if
it were there, and not there. Everyone

is giving the bear a wide berth.
But a crowd is gathering, too, bulging
out onto the Avenue. The man has
a chain around his waist. The chain
goes from his lap to the bear's collar,
a band of steel. On the table
in front of the man rests an iron bar
with a leather handle. And as if this
were not enough, the man drains the last
of his beer and picks up his bar.
Gets up from the table and hauls
on the chain. The bear stirs, opens its
mouth – old brown and yellow fangs.
But fangs. The man jerks on the chain,
hard. The bear rises to all fours now
and growls. The man slaps the bear on
its shoulder with the bar, bringing
a tiny cloud of dust. Growls something

himself. The bear waits while the man takes
another swing. Slowly, the bear rises
onto its hind legs, swings at air and at
that goddamned bar. Begins to shuffle
then, begins to snap its jaws as the man
slugs it again, and, yes, again

with that bar. There's a tamborine.
I nearly forgot that. The man shakes
it as he chants, as he strikes the bear
who weaves on its hind legs. Growls
and snaps and weaves in a poor dance.
This scene lasts forever. Whole seasons
come and go before it's over and the bear
drops to all fours. Sits down on its
haunches, gives a low, sad growl.
The man puts the tamborine on the table.
Puts the iron bar on the table, too.
Then he takes off his hat. No one
applauds. A few people see
what's coming and walk away. But not
before the hat appears at the edge
of the crowd and begins to make its
way from hand to hand
through the throng. The hat
comes to me and stops. I'm holding
the hat, and I can't believe it.
Everybody staring at it.
I stare right along with them.
You say my name, and in the same breath
hiss, "For God's sake, pass it along."
I toss in the money I have. Then
we leave and go on to the next thing.

Hours later, in bed, I touch you

and wait, and then touch you again.
Whereupon, you uncurl your fingers.
I put my hands all over you then –
your limbs, your long hair even, hair
that I touch and cover my face with,
and draw salt from. But later,
when I close my eyes, the hat
appears. Then the tamborine. The chain.

THE YOUNG FIRE EATERS
OF MEXICO CITY

They fill their mouths with alcohol
and blow it over a lighted candle
at traffic signs. Anyplace, really,
where cars line up and the drivers
are angry and frustrated and looking
for distraction – there you'll find
the young fire eaters. Doing what they do
for a few pesos. If they're lucky.
But in a year their lips
are scorched and their throats raw.
They have no voice within a year.
They can't talk or cry out –
these silent children who hunt
through the streets with a candle
and a beer can filled with alcohol.
They are called *milusos*. Which translates
into "a thousand uses".

POWDER-MONKEY

When my friend John Dugan, the carpenter,
left this world for the next, he seemed
in a terrible hurry. He wasn't, of course.
Almost no one is. But he barely took time
to say goodbye. "I'll just put these tools away,"
he said. Then, "So long." And hurried
down the hill to his pickup. He waved, and
I waved. But between here and Dungeness,
where he used to live, he drifted
over the center line, onto Death's side.
And was destroyed by a logging truck.

                        He is working
under the sun with his shirt off, a blue
bandanna around his forehead to keep sweat from his eyes.
Driving nails. Drilling and planing lumber.
Joining wood together with other wood.
In every way taking the measure of this house.
Stopping to tell a story now and then,
about when he was a young squirt, working
as a powder-monkey. The close calls he'd had
laying fuses. His white teeth flashing when he laughs.
The blond handlebar mustache he loved to
pull on while musing. "So long," he said.

I want to imagine him riding unharmed
towards Death. Even though the fuse is burning.
Nothing to do there in the cab
of his pickup but listen to Ricky Scaggs,
pull on his mustache, and plan Saturday night.

This man with all Death before him.
Riding unharmed, and untouched,
toward Death.

THE PEN

The pen that told the truth
went into the washing machine
for its trouble. Came out
an hour later, and was tossed
in the dryer with jeans
and a western shirt. Days passed
while it lay quietly on the desk
under the window. Lay there
thinking it was finished.
Without a single conviction
to its name. It didn't have
the will to go on, even if it'd wanted.
But one morning, an hour or so
before sunrise, it came to life
and wrote:
"The damp fields asleep in moonlight."
Then it was still again.
Its usefulness in this life
clearly at an end.

He shook it and whacked it
on the desk. Then gave up
on it, or nearly.
Once more though, with the greatest
effort, it summoned its last
reserves. This is what it wrote:
"A light wind, and beyond the window
trees swimming in the golden morning air."

He tried to write some more

but that was all. The pen
quit working forever.
By and by it was put
into the stove along with
other junk. And much later
it was another pen,
an undistinguished pen
that hadn't proved itself
yet, that facilely wrote:
"Darkness gathers in the branches.
Stay inside. Keep still."

THE PIPE

The next poem I write will have firewood
right in the middle of it, firewood so thick
with pitch my friend will leave behind
his gloves and tell me, "Wear these when you
handle that stuff." The next poem
will have night in it, too, and all the stars
in the Western Hemisphere; and an immense body
of water shining for miles under a new moon.
The next poem will have a bedroom
and living room for itself, skylights,
a sofa, a table and chairs by the window,
a vase of violets cut just an hour before lunch.
There'll be a lamp burning in the next poem;
and a fireplace where pitch-soaked
blocks of fir flame up, consuming one another.
Oh, the next poem will throw sparks!
But there won't be any cigarettes in that poem.
I'll take up smoking the pipe.

WHAT YOU NEED FOR PAINTING

from a letter by Renoir

THE PALETTE:

Flake white
Chrome yellow
Naples yellow
Yellow ocher
Raw umber
Venetian red
French vermilion
Madder lake

Rose madder
Cobalt blue
Ultramarine blue
Emerald green
Ivory black
Raw sienna
Viridian green
White lead

DON'T FORGET:
Palette knife
Scraping knife
Essence of turpentine

BRUSHES?
Pointed marten-hair brushes
Flat hog-hair brushes

Indifference to everything except your canvas.
The ability to work like a locomotive.
An iron will.

BONNARD'S NUDES

His wife. Forty years he painted her.
Again and again. The nude in the last painting
the same young nude as the first. His wife.

As he remembered her young. As she was young.
His wife in her bath. At her dressing table
in front of the mirror. Undressed.

His wife with her hands under her breasts
looking out on the garden.
The sun bestowing warmth and color.

Every living thing in bloom there.
She young and tremulous and most desirable.
When she died, he painted a while longer.

A few landscapes. Then died.
And was put down next to her.
His young wife.

A SQUALL

Shortly after three P.M. today a squall
hit the calm waters of the Strait.
A black cloud moving fast,
carrying rain, driven by high winds.

The water rose up and turned white.
Then, in five minutes, was as before –
blue and most remarkable, with just
a little chop. It occurs to me
it was this kind of squall
that came upon Shelley and his friend,
Williams, in the Gulf of Spezia, on
an otherwise fine day. There they were,
running ahead of a smart breeze,
wind-jamming, crying out to each other,
I want to think, in sheer exuberance.
In Shelley's jacket pockets, Keats's poems,
and a volume of Sophocles!
Then something like smoke on the water.
A black cloud moving fast,
carrying rain, driven by high winds.

Black cloud
hastening along the end
of the first romantic period
in English poetry.

KAFKA'S WATCH

from a letter

I have a job with a tiny salary of 80 crowns, and
an infinite eight to nine hours of work.
I devour the time outside the office like a wild beast.
Someday I hope to sit in a chair in another
country, looking out the window at fields of sugarcane
or Mohammedan cemeteries.
I don't complain about the work so much as about
the sluggishness of swampy time. The office hours
cannot be divided up! I feel the pressure
of the full eight or nine hours even in the last
half hour of the day. It's like a train ride
lasting night and day. In the end you're totally
crushed. You no longer think about the straining
of the engine, or about the hills or
flat countryside, but ascribe all that's happening
to your watch alone. The watch which you continually hold
in the palm of your hand. Then shake. And bring slowly
to your ear in disbelief.

MY WORK

I look up and see them starting
down the beach. The young man
is wearing a packboard to carry the baby.
This leaves his hands free
so that he can take one of his wife's hands
in his, and swing his other. Anyone can see
how happy they are. And intimate. How steady.
They are happier than anyone else, and they know it.
Are gladdened by it, and humbled.
They walk to the end of the beach
and out of sight. That's it, I think,
and return to this thing governing
my life. But in a few minutes

they come walking back along the beach.
The only thing different
is that they have changed sides.
He is on the other side of her now,
the ocean side. She is on this side.
But they are still holding hands. Even more
in love, if that's possible. And it is.
Having been there for a long time myself.
Theirs has been a modest walk, fifteen minutes
down the beach, fifteen minutes back.
They've had to pick their way
over some rocks and around huge logs,
tossed up from when the sea ran wild.

They walk quietly, slowly, holding hands.

They know the water is out there
but they're so happy that they ignore it.
The love in their young faces. The surround of it.
Maybe it *will* last forever. If they are lucky,
and good, and forebearing. And careful. If they
go on loving each other without stint.
Are true to each other – that most of all.
As they will be, of course, as they will be,
as they know they will be.
I go back to my work. My work goes back to me.
A wind picks up out over the water.

THE GARDEN

In the garden, small laughter from years ago.
Lanterns burning in the willows.
The power of those four words, "I loved a woman."
Put that on the stone beside his name.
God keep you and be with you.

Those horses coming into the stretch at Ruidoso!
Mist rising from the meadow at dawn.
From the veranda, the blue outlines of the mountains.
What used to be within reach, out of reach.
And in some lesser things, just the opposite is true.

Order anything you want! Then look for the man
with the limp to go by. He'll pay.
From a break in the wall, I could look down
on the shanty lights in the Valley of Kidron.
Very little sleep under strange roofs. His life far away.

Playing checkers with my dad. Then he hunts up
the shaving soap, the brush and bowl, the straight
razor, and we drive to the county hospital. I watch him
lather my grandpa's face. Then shave him.
The dying body is a clumsy partner.

Drops of water in your hair.
The dark yellow of the fields, the black and blue rivers.
Going out for a walk means you intend to return, right?
Eventually.
The flame is guttering. Marvelous.

The meeting between Goethe and Beethoven
took place in Leipzig in 1812. They talked into the night
about Lord Byron and Napoleon.
She got off the road and from then on it was nothing
but hardpan all the way.

She took a stick and in the dust drew the house where
they'd live and raise their children.
There was a duck pond and a place for horses.
To write about it, one would have to write in a way
that would stop the heart and make one's hair stand on end.

Cervantes lost a hand in the Battle of Lepanto.
This was in 1571, the last great sea battle fought
in ships manned by galley slaves.
In the Unuk River, in Ketchikan, the backs of the salmon
under the street lights as they come through town.

Students and young people chanted a requiem
as Tolstoy's coffin was carried across the yard
of the stationmaster's house at Astapovo and placed
in the freight car. To the accompaniment of singing,
the train slowly moved off.

A hard sail and the same stars everywhere.
But the garden is right outside my window.
Don't worry your heart about me, my darling.
We weave the thread given to us.
And Spring is with me.

MY CROW

A crow flew into the tree outside my window.
It was not Ted Hughes's crow, or Galway's crow.
Or Frost's, Pasternak's, or Lorca's crow.
Or one of Homer's crows, stuffed with gore,
after the battle. This was just a crow.
That never fit in anywhere in its life,
or did anything worth mentioning.
It sat there on the branch for a few minutes.
Then picked up and flew beautifully
out of my life.

GRIEF

Woke up early this morning and from my bed
looked far across the Strait to see
a small boat moving through the choppy water,
a single running light on. Remembered
my friend who used to shout
his dead wife's name from hilltops
around Perugia. Who set a plate
for her at his simple table long after
she was gone. And opened the windows
so she could have fresh air. Such display
I found embarrassing. So did his other
friends. I couldn't see it.
Not until this morning.

BAHIA, BRAZIL

The wind is level now. But pails of rain
fell today, and the day before,
and the day before that, all the way back
to Creation. The buildings
in the old slave quarter are dissolving,
and nobody cares. Not the ghosts
of the old slaves, or the young.
The water feels good on their whipped backs.
They could cry with relief.

No sunsets in this place. Light one minute,
and then the stars come out.
We could look all night in vain
for the Big Dipper. Down here
the Southern Cross is our sign.
I'm sick of the sound of my own voice!
Uneasy, and dreaming
of rum that could split my skull open.

There's a body lying on the stairs.
Step over it. The lights in the tower
have gone out. A spider hops from the man's
hair. This life. I'm saying it's one
amazing thing after the other.

Lines of men in the street,
as opposed to lines of poetry.
Choose! Are you guilty or not guilty?
What else have you? he answered.
Well, say the house was burning.

Would you save the cat or the Rembrandt?
That's easy. I don't have a Rembrandt,
and I don't have a cat. But I have
a sorrel horse back home
that I want to ride once more
into the high country.

Soon enough we'll rot under the earth.
No truth to this, just a fact.
We who gave each other so much
happiness while alive –
we're going to rot. But we won't
rot in this place. Not here.
Arms shackled together.
Jesus, the very idea of such a thing!
This life. These shackles.
I shouldn't bring it up.

THE HOUSE BEHIND THIS ONE

The afternoon was already dark and unnatural.
When this old woman appeared in the field,
in the rain, carrying a bridle.
She came up the road to the house.
The house behind this one. Somehow
she knew Antonio Ríos had entered
the hour of his final combat.
Somehow, don't ask me how, she knew.

The doctor and some other people were with him.
But nothing more could be done. And so
the old woman carried the bridle into the room,
and hung it across the foot of his bed.
The bed where he writhed and lay dying.
She went away without a word.
This woman who'd once been young and beautiful.
When Antonio was young and beautiful.

READING

Every man's life is a mystery, even as
yours is, and mine. Imagine
a château with a window opening
onto Lake Geneva. There in the window
on warm and sunny days is a man
so engrossed in reading he doesn't look
up. Or if he does he marks his place
with a finger, raises his eyes, and peers
across the water to Mont Blanc,
and beyond, to Selah, Washington,
where he is with a girl
and getting drunk *for the first time*.
The last thing he remembers, before
he passes out, is that she spit on him.
He keeps on drinking
and getting spit on for years.
But some people will tell you
that suffering is good for the character.
You're free to believe anything.
In any case, he goes
back to reading and will not
feel guilty about his mother
drifting in her boat of sadness,
or consider his children
and their troubles that go on and on.
Nor does he intend to think about
the clear-eyed woman he once loved
and her defeat at the hands of eastern religion.
Her grief has no beginning, and no end.

Let anyone in the château, or Selah,
come forward who might claim kin with the man
who sits all day in the window reading,
like a picture of a man reading.
Let the sun come forward.
Let the man himself come forward.
What in Hell can he be reading?

EVENING

I fished alone that languid autumn evening.
Fished as darkness kept coming on.
Experiencing exceptional loss and then
exceptional joy when I brought a silver salmon
to the boat, and dipped a net under the fish.
Secret heart! When I looked into the moving water
and up at the dark outline of the mountains
behind the town, nothing hinted then
I would suffer so this longing
to be back once more, before I die.
Far from everything, and far from myself.

SPELL

Between five and seven this evening,
I lay in the channel of sleep. Attached
to this world by nothing more than hope,
I turned in a current of dark dreams.
It was during this time the weather
underwent a metamorphosis.
Became deranged. What before had been
vile and shabby, but comprehensible,
became swollen and
unrecognizable. Something utterly vicious.

In my despairing mood, I didn't
need it. It was the last thing on earth
I wanted. So with all the power I could muster,
I sent it packing. Sent it down the coast
to a big river I know about. A river
able to deal with foul weather
like this. So what if the river has to flee
to higher ground? Give it a few days.
It'll find its way.

Then all will be as before. I swear
this won't be more than a bad memory, if that.
Why, this time next week I won't remember
what I was feeling when I wrote this.
I'll have forgotten I slept badly
and dreamed for a time this evening . . .
to wake at seven o'clock, look out
at the storm and, after that first shock –

take heart. Think long and hard
about what I want, what I could let go
or send away. And then do it!
Like that. With words, and signs.

THE SCHOOLDESK

The fishing in Lough Arrow is piss-poor.
Too much rain, too much high water.
They say the mayfly hatch has come
and gone. All day I stay put
by the window of the borrowed cottage
in Ballindoon, waiting for a break
in the weather. A turf fire smokes
in the grate, though no romance
in this or anything else
here. Just outside the window an old iron
and wood schooldesk keeps me company.
Something is carved into the desk under
the inkwell. It doesn't matter
what; I'm not curious. It's enough
to imagine the instrument
that gouged those letters.

       My dad is dead,
and Mother slips in and out of her mind.
I can't begin to say how bad it is
for my grown-up son and daughter.
They took one long look at me
and tried to make all my mistakes.
More's the pity. Bad luck for them,
my sweet children. And haven't I mentioned
my first wife yet? What's wrong with me
that I haven't? Well, I can't anymore.
Shouldn't, anyway. She claims
I say too much as it is.
Says she's happy now, and grinds her teeth.

Says the Lord Jesus loves her,
and she'll get by. That love
of my life over and done with. But what
does that say about my life?
My loved ones are thousands of miles away.
But they're in this cottage too,
in Ballindoon. And in every
hotel room I wake up in these days.

The rain has let up.
And the sun has appeared and small
clouds of unexpected mayflies,
proving someone wrong. We move
to the door in a group, my family and I.
And go outside. Where I bend over the desk
and run my fingers across its rough surface.
Someone laughs, someone grinds her teeth.
And someone, someone is pleading with me.
Saying, "For Christ's sake, don't
turn your back on me."

An ass and cart pass down the lane.
The driver takes the pipe from his mouth
and raises his hand.
There's the smell of lilacs in the damp air.
Mayflies hover over the lilacs,
and over the heads of my loved ones.
Hundreds of mayflies.
I sit on the bench. Lean
over the desk. I can remember
myself with a pen. In the beginning,
looking at pictures of words.
Learning to write them, slowly,
one letter at a time. Pressing down.
A word. Then the next.

The feeling of mastering something.
The excitement of it.
Pressing hard. At first
the damage confined to the surface.
But then deeper.

These blossoms. Lilacs.
How they fill the air with sweetness!
Mayflies in the air as the cart
goes by – as the fish rise.

FIVE

AFTER RAINY DAYS

After rainy days and the same serious doubts –
strange to walk past the golf course,
sun overhead, men putting, or teeing, whatever
they do on those green links. To the river that flows
past the clubhouse. Expensive houses on either side
of the river, a dog barking at this kid
who revs his motorcycle. To see a man fighting
a large salmon in the water just below
the footbridge. Where a couple of joggers have stopped
to watch. Never in my life have I seen anything
like this! Stay with him, I think, breaking
into a run. For Christ's sake, man, hold on!

HOMINY AND RAIN

In a little patch of ground beside
the wall of the Earth Sciences building,
a man in a canvas hat was on
his knees doing something in the rain
with some plants. Piano music
came from an upstairs window
in the building next door. Then
the music stopped.
And the window was brought down.

You told me those white blossoms
on the cherry trees in the Quad
smelled like a can of just-opened
hominy. Hominy. They reminded you
of that. This may or may not
be true. I can't say.
I've lost my sense of smell,
along with any interest I may ever
have expressed in working
on my knees with plants, or
vegetables. There was a barefoot

madman with a ring in his ear
playing his guitar and singing
reggae. I remember that.
Rain puddling around his feet.
The place he'd picked to stand
had Welcome Fear
painted on the sidewalk in red letters.

At the time it seemed important
to recall the man on his knees
in front of his plants.
The blossoms. Music of one kind,
and another. Now I'm not so sure.
I can't say, for sure.

It's a little like some tiny cave-in,
in my brain. There's a sense
that I've lost – not everything,
not everything, but far too much.
A part of my life forever.
Like hominy.

Even though your arm stayed linked
in mine. Even though that. Even
though we stood quietly in the
doorway as the rain picked up.
And watched it without saying
anything. Stood quietly.
At peace, I think. Stood watching
the rain. While the one
with the guitar played on.

RADIO WAVES

for Antonio Machado

This rain has stopped, and the moon has come out.
I don't understand the first thing about radio
waves. But I think they travel better just after
a rain, when the air is damp. Anyway, I can reach out
now and pick up Ottawa, if I want to, or Toronto.
Lately, at night, I've found myself
becoming slightly interested in Canadian politics
and domestic affairs. It's true. But mostly it was their
music stations I was after. I could sit here in the chair
and listen, without having to do anything, or think.
I don't have a TV, and I'd quit reading
the papers. At night I turned on the radio.

When I came out here I was trying to get away
from everything. Especially literature.
What that entails, and what comes after.
There is in the soul a desire for not thinking.
For being still. Coupled with this
a desire to be strict, yes, and rigorous.
But the soul is also a smooth son of a bitch,
not always trustworthy. And I forgot that.
I listened when it said, Better to sing that which is gone
and will not return than that which is still
with us and will be with us tomorrow. Or not.
And if not, that's all right too.
It didn't much matter, it said, if a man sang at all.
That's the voice I listened to.
Can you imagine somebody thinking like this?
That it's really all one and the same?
What nonsense!

But I'd think these stupid thoughts at night
as I sat in the chair and listened to my radio.

Then, Machado, your poetry!
It was a little like a middle-aged man falling
in love again. A remarkable thing to witness,
and embarrassing, too.
Silly things like putting your picture up.
And I took your book to bed with me
and slept with it near at hand. A train went by
in my dreams one night and woke me up.
And the first thing I thought, heart racing
there in the dark bedroom, was this —
It's all right, Machado is here.
Then I could fall back to sleep again.

Today I took your book with me when I went
for my walk. "Pay attention!" you said,
when anyone asked what to do with their lives.
So I looked around and made note of everything.
Then sat down with it in the sun, in my place
beside the river where I could see the mountains.
And I closed my eyes and listened to the sound
of the water. Then I opened them and began to read
"Abel Martin's Last Lamentations."
This morning I thought about you hard, Machado.
And I hope, even in the face of what I know about death,
that you got the message I intended.
But it's okay even if you didn't. Sleep well. Rest.
Sooner or later I hope we'll meet.
And then I can tell you these things myself.

THE PHENOMENON

I woke up feeling wiped out. God knows
where I've been all night, but my feet hurt.
Outside my window, a phenomenon is taking place.
The sun and moon hang side-by-side over the water.
Two sides of the same coin. I climb from bed
slowly, much as an old man might maneuver
from his musty bed in midwinter, finding it difficult
for a moment even to make water! I tell myself
this has to be a temporary condition.
In a few years, no problem. But when I look out
the window again, there's a sudden swoop of feeling.
Once more I'm arrested with the beauty of this place.
I was lying if I ever said anything to the contrary.
I move closer to the glass and see it's happened
between this thought and that. The moon
is gone. Set, at last.

FEAR

Fear of seeing a police car pull into the drive.
Fear of falling asleep at night.
Fear of not falling asleep.
Fear of the past rising up.
Fear of the present taking flight.
Fear of the telephone that rings in the dead of night.
Fear of electrical storms.
Fear of the cleaning woman who has a spot on her cheek!
Fear of dogs I've been told won't bite.
Fear of anxiety!
Fear of having to identify the body of a dead friend.
Fear of running out of money.
Fear of having too much, though people will not believe this.
Fear of psychological profiles.
Fear of being late and fear of arriving before anyone else.
Fear of my children's handwriting on envelopes.
Fear they'll die before I do, and I'll feel guilty.
Fear of having to live with my mother in her old age, and mine.
Fear of confusion.
Fear this day will end on an unhappy note.
Fear of waking up to find you gone.
Fear of not loving and fear of not loving enough.
Fear that what I love will prove lethal to those I love.
Fear of death.
Fear of living too long.
Fear of death.
     I've said that.

THE MAIL

On my desk, a picture postcard from my son
in southern France. The Midi,
he calls it. Blue skies. Beautiful houses
loaded with begonias. Nevertheless
he's going under, needs money fast.

Next to his card, a letter
from my daughter telling me her old man,
the speed-freak, is tearing down
a motorcycle in the living room.
They're existing on oatmeal,
she and her children. For God's sake,
she could use some help.

And there's the letter from my mother
who is sick and losing her mind.
She tells me she won't be here
much longer. Won't I help her make
this one last move? Can't I pay
for her to have a home of her own?

I go outside. Thinking to walk
to the graveyard for some comfort.
But the sky is in turmoil.
The clouds, huge and swollen with darkness,
about to spew open.
It's then the postman turns into
the drive. His face
is a reptile's, glistening and working.

His hand goes back – as if to strike!
It's the mail.

EGRESS

I opened the old spiral notebook to see what I'd been
thinking in those days. There was one entry,
in a hand I didn't recognize as mine, but was mine.
All that paper I'd let go to waste back then!

Removing the door for Dr Kurbitz.

What on earth could that possibly mean to me,
or anyone, today? Then I went back
to that time. To just after being married. How I earned
our daily bread delivering for Al Kurbitz,
the pharmacist. Whose brother Ken – Dr Kurbitz
to me, the ear-nose-and-throat man – fell dead
one night after dinner, after
talking over some business deal. He died in the bathroom,
his body wedged between the door and toilet stool.
Blocking the way. First the *whump*
of a body hitting the floor, and then Mr Kurbitz
and his snazzy sister-in-law shouting "Ken! Ken!"
and pushing on the bathroom door.

Mr Kurbitz had to take the door off its hinges
with a screwdriver. It saved the ambulance drivers
a minute, maybe. He said his brother never knew
what hit him. Dead before he hit the floor.

Since then, I've seen doors removed from their hinges
many times, with and without the aid of screwdrivers.
But I'd forgotten about Dr Kurbitz, and so much else

from that time. Never, until today, did I connect
this act with dying.

                              In those days, death,
if it happened, happened to others. Old people
belonging to my parents. Or else people of consequence.
People in a different income bracket, whose death
and removal had nothing to do with me, or mine.

We were living in Dr Coglon's basement
apartment, and I was in love for the first time
ever. My wife was pregnant. We were thrilled
beyond measure or accounting for, given our mean
surroundings. And that, I'm saying, may be why
I never wrote more about Dr Kurbitz,
his brother Al, or doors that had to be taken off
their hinges for the sake of dead people.

What the hell! Who needed death and notebooks? We
were young and happy. Death was coming, sure.
But for the old and worn-out. Or else people in books.
And, once in a while, the well-heeled professionals
I trembled before and said "Yes, Sir" to.

THE RIVER

I waded, deepening, into the dark water.
Evening, and the push
and swirl of the river as it closed
around my legs and held on.
Young grilse broke water.
Parr darted one way, smolt another.
Gravel turned under my boots as I edged out.
Watched by the furious eyes of king salmon.
Their immense heads turned slowly,
eyes burning with fury, as they hung
in the deep current.
They were there. I felt them there,
and my skin prickled. But
there was something else.
I braced with the wind on my neck.
Felt the hair rise
as something touched my boot.
Grew afraid at what I couldn't see.
Then of everything that filled my eyes –
that other shore heavy with branches,
the dark lip of the mountain range behind.
And this river that had suddenly
grown black and swift.
I drew breath and cast anyway.
Prayed nothing would strike.

MIGRATION

A late summer's day, and my friend on the court
with his friend. Between games, the other remarks
how my friend's step seems not to have any spring
to it. His serve isn't so hot, either.
"You feeling okay?" he asks. "You had a checkup
lately?" Summer, and the living is easy.
But my friend went to see a doctor friend of his.
Who took his arm and gave him three months, no longer.

When I saw him a day later, it
was in the afternoon. He was watching TV.
He looked the same, but — how should I say it? —
different. He was embarrassed about the TV
and turned the sound down a little. But he couldn't
sit still. He circled the room, again and again.
"It's a program on animal migration," he said, as if this
might explain everything.
I put my arms around him and gave him a hug.
Not the really big hug I was capable of. Being afraid
that one of us, or both, might go to pieces.
And there was the momentary, crazy and dishonorable
    thought —
this might be catching.

I asked for an ashtray, and he was happy
to range around the house until he found one.
We didn't talk. Not then. Together we finished watching
the show. Reindeer, polar bears, fish, waterfowl,
butterflies and more. Sometimes they went from one
continent, or ocean, to another. But it was hard

161

to pay attention to the story taking place on screen.
My friend stood, as I recall, the whole time.

Was he feeling okay? He felt fine. He just couldn't
seem to stay still, was all. Something came into his eyes
and went away again. "What in hell are they talking about?"
he wanted to know. But didn't wait for an answer.
Began to walk some more. I followed him awkwardly
from room to room while he remarked on the weather,
his job, his ex-wife, his kids. Soon, he guessed,
he'd have to tell them . . . something.
"Am I really going to die?"

What I remember most about that awful day
was his restlessness, and my cautious hugs – *hello, goodbye*.
He kept moving until
we reached the front door and stopped.
He peered out, and drew back as if astounded
it could be light outside. A bank of shadow
from his hedge blocked the drive. And shadow fell
from the garage onto his lawn. He walked me to the car.
Our shoulders bumped. We shook hands, and I hugged him
once more. Lightly. Then he turned and went back,
passing quickly inside, closing the door. His face
appeared behind the window, then was gone.

He'll be on the move from now on. Traveling night and day,
without cease, all of him, every last exploding piece
of him. Until he reaches a place only he knows about.
An Arctic place, cold and frozen. Where he thinks,
This is far enough. This is the place.
And lies down, for he is tired.

SLEEPING

He slept on his hands.
On a rock.
On his feet.
On someone else's feet.
He slept on buses, trains, in airplanes.
Slept on duty.
Slept beside the road.
Slept on a sack of apples.
He slept in a pay toilet.
In a hayloft.
In the Super Dome.
Slept in a Jaguar, and in the back of a pickup.
Slept in theaters.
In jail.
On boats.
He slept in line shacks and, once, in a castle.
Slept in the rain.
In blistering sun he slept.
On horseback.
He slept in chairs, churches, in fancy hotels.
He slept under strange roofs all his life.
Now he sleeps under the earth.
Sleeps on and on.
Like an old king.

AN ACCOUNT

He began the poem at the kitchen table,
one leg crossed over the other.
He wrote for a time, as if
only half interested in the result. It wasn't
as if the world didn't have enough poems.
The world had plenty of poems. Besides,
he'd been away for months.
He hadn't even *read* a poem in months.
What kind of life was this? A life
where a man was too busy even to read poems?
No life at all. Then he looked out the window,
down the hill to Frank's house.
A nice house situated near the water.
He remembered Frank opening his door
every morning at nine o'clock.
Going out for his walks.
He drew nearer the table, and uncrossed his legs.

Last night he'd heard an account
of Frank's death from Ed, another neighbor.
A man the same age as Frank,
and Frank's good friend. Frank
and his wife watching TV. *Hill Street Blues.*
Frank's favorite show. When he gasps
twice, is thrown back in his chair –
"as if he'd been electrocuted." That fast,
he was dead. His color draining away.
He was gray, turning black. Betty runs
out of the house in her robe. Runs
to a neighbor's house where a girl knows

something about CPR. *She's* watching
the same show! They run back
to Frank's house. Frank totally black now,
in his chair in front of the TV.
The cops and other desperate characters
moving across the screen, raising their voices,
yelling at each other, while this neighbor girl
hauls Frank out of his chair onto the floor.
Tears open his shirt. Goes to work.
Frank being the first real–life victim
she's ever had.

                    She places her lips
on Frank's icy lips. A dead man's lips. Black lips.
And black his face and hands and arms.
Black too his chest where the shirt's been torn,
exposing the sparse hairs that grew there.
Long after she must've known better, she goes on
with it. Pressing her lips against his
unresponsive lips. Then stopping to beat on him
with clenched fists. Pressing her lips to his again,
and then again. Even after it's too late and it
was clear he wasn't coming back, she went on with it.
This girl, beating on him with her fists, calling
him every name she could think of. Weeping
when they took him away
from her. And someone thought to turn off
the images pulsing across the screen.

SIMPLE

A break in the clouds. The blue
outline of the mountains.
Dark yellow of the fields.
Black river. What am I doing here,
lonely and filled with remorse?

I go on casually eating from the bowl
of raspberries. If I were dead,
I remind myself, I wouldn't
be eating them. It's not so simple.
It is that simple.

SWEET LIGHT

After the winter, grieving and dull,
I flourished here all spring. Sweet light

began to fill my chest. I pulled up
a chair. Sat for hours in front of the sea.

Listened to the buoy and learned
to tell the difference between a bell,

and the sound of a bell. I wanted
everything behind me. I even wanted

to become inhuman. And I did that.
I know I did. (She'll back me up on this.)

I remember the morning I closed the lid
on memory and turned the handle.

Locking it away forever.
Nobody knows what happened to me

out here, sea. Only you and I know.
At night, clouds form in front of the moon.

By morning they're gone. And that sweet light
I spoke of? That's gone too.

LISTENING

It was a night like all the others. Empty
of everything save memory. He thought
he'd got to the other side of things.
But he hadn't. He read a little
and listened to the radio. Looked out the window
for a while. Then went upstairs. In bed
realized he'd left the radio on.
But closed his eyes anyway. Inside the deep night,
as the house sailed west, he woke up
to hear voices murmuring. And froze.
Then understood it was only the radio.
He got up and went downstairs. He had
to pee anyway. A little rain
that hadn't been there before was
falling outside. The voices
on the radio faded and then came back
as if from a long way. It wasn't
the same station any longer. A man's voice
said something about Borodin,
and his opera *Prince Igor*. The woman
he said this to agreed, and laughed.
Began to tell a little of the story.
The man's hand drew back from the switch.
Once more he found himself in the presence
of mystery. Rain. Laughter. History.
Art. The hegemony of death.
He stood there, listening.

THE EVE OF BATTLE

There are five of us in the tent, not counting
the batman cleaning my rifle. There's
a lively argument going on amongst my brother
officers. In the cookpot, salt pork turns
alongside some macaroni. But these fine fellows
aren't hungry – and it's a good thing!
All they want is to harrumph about the likes
of Huss and Hegel, anything to pass the time.
Who cares? Tomorrow we fight. Tonight they want
to sit around and chatter about nothing, about
philosophy. Maybe the cookpot isn't there
for them? Nor the stove, or those folding
stools they're sitting on. Maybe there isn't
a battle waiting for them tomorrow morning?
We'd all like that best. Maybe
I'm not there for them, either. Ready
to dish up something to eat. *Un est autre*,
as someone said. I, or another, may as well be
in China. Time to eat, brothers,
I say, handing round the plates. But someone
has just ridden up and dismounted. My batman
moves to the door of the tent, then drops his plate
and steps back. Death walks in without saying
anything, dressed in coat-and-tails.
At first I think he must be looking for the Emperor,
who's old and ailing anyway. That would explain
it. Death's lost his way. What else could it be?
He has a slip of paper in his hand, looks us over
quickly, consults some names.
He raises his eyes. I turn to the stove.

When I turn back, everyone has gone. Everyone
except Death. He's still there, unmoving.
I give him his plate. He's come a long
way. He is hungry, I think, and will eat anything.

THE CAUCASUS: A ROMANCE

Each evening an eagle soars down from the snowy
crags and passes over camp. It wants to see
if it's true what they say back in Russia: the only
career open to young men these days
is the military. Young men of good family, and a few
others – older, silent men – men who've blotted their
copybooks, as they call it out here. Men like
the Colonel, who lost his ear in a duel.

Dense forests of pine, alder, and birch. Torrents
that fall from dizzying precipices. Mist. Clamorous
rivers. Mountains covered with snow even now, even
in August. Everywhere, as far as the eye can reach,
profusion. A sea of poppies. Wild buckwheat that
shimmers in the heat, that waves and rolls to the horizon.
Panthers. Bees as big as a boy's fist. Bears that won't
get out of a man's way, that will tear a body to
pieces and then go back to the business of rooting
and chuffing like hogs in the rich undergrowth. Clouds
of white butterflies that rise, then settle and
rise again on slopes thick with lilac and fern.

Now and then a real engagement with the enemy.
Much howling from their side, cries, the drum
of horses' hooves, rattle of musket fire, a Chechen's ball
smashing into a man's breast, a stain that blossoms
and spreads, that ripples over the white uniform like crimson
petals opening. Then the chase begins: hearts racing,
minds emptying out entirely as the Emperor's young
men, dandies all, gallop over plains, laughing,

yelling their lungs out. Or else they urge
their lathered horses along forest trails, pistols
ready. They burn Chechen crops, kill Chechen stock,
knock down the pitiful villages. They're soldiers,
after all, and these are not maneuvers. Shamil,
the bandit chieftain, he's the one they want most.

At night, a moon broad and deep as a serving dish
sallies out from behind the peaks. But this
moon is only for appearance's sake. Really, it's
armed to the teeth, like everything else out here.
When the Colonel sleeps, he dreams of a drawing room –
one drawing room in particular – oh, clean and elegant,
most comfortable drawing room! Where friends lounge
in plush chairs, or on divans, and drink from
little glasses of tea. In the dream, it is always
Thursday, 2–4. There is a piano next to the window
that looks out on Nevsky Prospect. A young woman
finishes playing, pauses, and turns to the polite
applause. But in the dream it is the Circassian
woman with a saber cut across her face. His friends
draw back in horror. They lower their eyes, bow,
and begin taking their leave. Goodbye, goodbye,
they mutter. In Petersburg they said that out here,
in the Caucasus, sunsets are everything.
But this is not true; sunsets are not enough.
In Petersburg they said the Caucasus is a country that gives
rise to legend, where heroes are born every day.
They said, long ago, in Petersburg, that reputations
were made, and lost, in the Caucasus. *A gravely
beautiful place*, as one of the Colonel's men put it.

The officers serving under him will return
home soon, and more young men will come to take
their places. After the new arrivals dismount

to pay their respects, the Colonel will keep them
waiting a time. Then fix them with a stern but
fatherly gaze, these slim young men with tiny
mustaches and boisterous high spirits, who look
at him and wonder, who ask themselves what it is
he's running from. But he's not running. He likes it
here, in the Caucasus, after a fashion. He's even
grown used to it – or nearly. There's plenty to do,
God knows. Plenty of grim work in the days, and months,
ahead. Shamil is out there in the mountains somewhere –
or maybe he's on the Steppes. The scenery is lovely,
you can be sure, and this but a rough record
of the actual and the passing.

THE REST

Clouds hang loosely over this mountain range
behind my house. In a while, the light
will go and the wind come up
to scatter these clouds, or some others,
across the sky.
                    I drop to my knees,
roll the big salmon onto its side
on the wet grass, and begin to use
the knife I was born with. Soon
I'll be at the table in the living room,
trying to raise the dead. The moon
and the dark water my companions.
My hands are silvery with scales.
Fingers mingling with the dark blood.
Finally, I cut loose the massive head.
I bury what needs burying
and keep the rest. Take one last look
at the high blue light. Turn
toward my house. My night.

SIX

LOCKING YOURSELF OUT
THEN TRYING TO GET BACK IN

You simply go out and shut the door
without thinking. And when you look back
at what you've done
it's too late. If this sounds
like the story of a life, okay.

It was raining. The neighbors who had
a key were away. I tried and tried
the lower windows. Stared
inside at the sofa, plants, the table
and chairs, the stereo set-up.
My coffee cup and ashtray waited for me
on the glass-topped table, and my heart
went out to them. I said, *Hello, friends*,
or something like that. After all,
this wasn't so bad.
Worse things had happened. This
was even a little funny. I found the ladder.
Took that and leaned it against the house.
Then climbed in the rain to the deck,
swung myself over the railing
and tried the door. Which was locked,
of course. But I looked in just the same
at my desk, some papers, and my chair.
This was the window on the other side
of the desk where I'd raise my eyes
and stare out when I sat at that desk.
This is not like downstairs, I thought.
This is something else.

And it was something to look in like that, unseen,
from the deck. To be there, inside, and not be there.
I don't even think I can talk about it.
I brought my face close to the glass
and imagined myself inside,
sitting at the desk. Looking up
from my work now and again.
Thinking about some other place
and some other time.
The people I had loved then.

I stood there for a minute in the rain.
Considering myself to be the luckiest of men.
Even though a wave of grief passed through me.
Even though I felt violently ashamed
of the injury I'd done back then.
I bashed that beautiful window.
And stepped back in.

THE OLD DAYS

You'd dozed in front of the TV
but you hadn't been to bed yet
when you called. I was asleep,
or nearly, when the phone rang.
You wanted to tell me you'd thrown
a party. And I was missed.
It was like the old days, you
said, and laughed.
Dinner was a disaster.
Everybody dead drunk by the time
food hit the table. People
were having a good time, a great
time, a hell of a time, until
somebody took somebody
else's fiancée upstairs. Then
somebody pulled a knife.

But you got in front of the guy
as he was going upstairs
and talked him down.
Disaster narrowly averted,
you said, and laughed again.
You didn't remember much else
of what happened after that.
People got into their coats
and began to leave. You
must have dropped off for a few
minutes in front of the TV
because it was screaming at you
to get it a drink when you woke up.

Anyway, you're in Pittsburgh,
and I'm in here in this
little town on the other side
of the country. Most everyone
has cleared out of our lives now.
You wanted to call me up and say hello.
To say you were thinking
about me, and of the old days.
To say you were missing me.

It was then I remembered
back to those days and how
telephones used to jump when they rang.
And the people who would come
in those early-morning hours
to pound on the door in alarm.
Never mind the alarm felt inside.
I remembered that, and gravy dinners.
Knives lying around, waiting
for trouble. Going to bed
and hoping I wouldn't wake up.

I love you, Bro, you said.
And then a sob passed
between us. I took hold
of the receiver as if
it were my buddy's arm.
And I wished for us both
I could put my arms
around you, old friend.
I love you too, Bro.
I said that, and then we hung up.

MESOPOTAMIA

Waking before sunrise, in a house not my own,
I hear a radio playing in the kitchen.
Mist drifts outside the window while
a woman's voice gives the news, and then the weather.
I hear that, and the sound of meat
as it connects with hot grease in the pan.
I listen some more, half asleep. It's like,
but not like, when I was a child and lay in bed,
in the dark, listening to a woman crying,
and a man's voice raised in anger, or despair,
the radio playing all the while. Instead,
what I hear this morning is the man of the house
saying "How many summers do I have left?
Answer me that." There's no answer from the woman
that I can hear. But what *could* she answer,
given such a question? In a minute,
I hear his voice speaking of someone who I think
must be long gone: "That man could say,
   'O, Mesopotamia!'
and move his audience to tears."
I get out of bed at once and draw on my pants.
Enough light in the room that I can see
where I am, finally. I'm a grown man, after all,
and these people are my friends. Things
are not going well for them just now. Or else
they're going better than ever
because they're up early and talking
about such things of consequence
as death and Mesopotamia. In any case,
I feel myself being drawn to the kitchen.

So much that is mysterious and important
is happening out there this morning.

THE POSSIBLE

I spent years, on and off, in academe.
Taught at places I couldn't get near
as a student. But never wrote a line
about that time. Never. Nothing stayed
with me in those days. I was a stranger,
and an impostor, even to myself. Except
at that one school. That distinguished
institution in the midwest. Where
my only friend, and my colleague,
the Chaucerian, was arrested for beating his wife.
And threatening her life over the phone,
a misdemeanor. He wanted to put her eyes out.
Set her on fire for cheating.
The guy she was seeing, he was going to hammer him
into the ground like a fence post.

He lost his mind for a time, while she moved away
to a new life. Thereafter, he taught
his classes weeping drunk. More than once
wore his lunch on his shirt front.
I was no help. I was fading fast myself.
But seeing the way he was living, so to speak,
I understood I hadn't strayed so far from home
after all. My scholar-friend. My old pal.
At long last I'm out of all that.
And you. I pray your hands are steady,
and that you're happy tonight. I hope some woman
has just put her hand under your clean collar
a minute ago, and told you she loves you.

Believe her, if you can, for it's possible she means it.
Is someone who will be true, and kind to you.
All your remaining days.

WAITING

Left off the highway and
down the hill. At the
bottom, hang another left.
Keep bearing left. The road
will make a Y. Left again.
There's a creek on the left.
Keep going. Just before
the road ends, there'll be
another road. Take it
and no other. Otherwise,
your life will be ruined
forever. There's a log house
with a shake roof, on the left.
It's not that house. It's
the next house, just over
a rise. The house
where trees are laden with
fruit. Where phlox, forsythia,
and marigold grow. It's
the house where the woman
stands in the doorway
wearing sun in her hair. The one
who's been waiting
all this time.
The woman who loves you.
The one who can say,
"What's kept you?"

IN SWITZERLAND

First thing to do in Zurich
is take the No. 5 "Zoo" trolley
to the end of the track,
and get off. Been warned about
the lions. How their roars
carry over from the zoo compound
to the Flutern Cemetery.
Where I walk along
the very beautiful path
to James Joyce's grave.
Always the family man, he's here
with his wife, Nora, of course.
And his son, Giorgio,
who died a few years ago.
Lucia, his daughter, his sorrow,
still alive, still confined
in an institution for the insane.
When she was brought the news
of her father's death, she said:
What is he doing under the ground, that idiot?
When will he decide to come out?
He's watching us all the time.
I lingered a while. I think
I said something aloud to Mr Joyce.
I must have. I know I must have.
But I don't recall what,
now, and I'll have to leave it at that.

A week later to the day, we depart
Zurich by train for Lucerne.

But early that morning I take
the No. 5 trolley once more
to the end of the line.
The roar of the lions falls over
the cemetery, as before.
The grass has been cut.
I sit on it for a while and smoke.
Just feels good to be there,
close to the grave. I didn't
have to say anything this time.

That night we gambled at the tables
at the Grand Hotel-Casino
on the very shore of Lake Lucerne.
Took in a strip show later.
But what to do with the memory
of that grave that came to me
in the midst of the show,
under the muted, pink stage light?
Nothing to do about it.
Or about the desire that came later,
crowding everything else out,
like a wave.
Still later, we sat on a bench
under some linden trees, under stars.
Made love with each other.
Reaching into each other's clothes for it.
The lake a few steps away.
Afterwards, dipped our hands
into the cold water.
Then walked back to our hotel,
happy and tired, ready to sleep
for eight hours.

All of us, all of us, all of us

trying to save
our immortal souls, some ways
seemingly more round-
about and mysterious
than others. We're having
a good time here. But hope
all will be revealed soon.

ASK HIM

Reluctantly, my son goes with me
through the iron gates
of the cemetery in Montparnasse.
"What a way to spend a day in Paris!"
is what he'd like to say. Did, in fact, say.
He speaks French. Has started a conversation
with a white-haired guard who offers himself
as our informal guide. So we move slowly,
the three of us, along row upon row of graves.
Everyone, it seems, is here.

It's quiet, and hot, and the street sounds
of Paris can't reach. The guard wants to steer us
to the grave of the man who invented the submarine,
and Maurice Chevalier's grave. And the grave
of the 28-year-old singer, Nonnie,
covered with a mound of red roses.

I want to see the graves of the writers.
My son sighs. He doesn't want to see any of it.
Has seen enough. He's passed beyond boredom
into resignation. Guy de Maupassant; Sartre; Sainte-Beuve;
Gautier; the Goncourts; Paul Verlaine and his old comrade,
Charles Baudelaire. Where we linger.

None of these names, or graves, have anything to do
with the regulated lives of my son and the guard.
Who can this morning talk and joke together
in the French language under a fine sun.

But there are several names chiseled on Baudelaire's stone,
and I can't understand why.

Charles Baudelaire's name is between that of his mother,
who loaned him money and worried all her life
about his health, and his stepfather, a martinet
he hated and who hated him and everything he stood for.
"Ask your friend," I say. So my son asks.
It's as if he and the guard are old friends now,
and I'm there to be humored.
The guard says something and then lays
one hand over the other. Like that. Does it
again. One hand over the other. Grinning. Shrugging.
My son translates. But I understand.
"Like a sandwich, Pop," my son says. "A Baudelaire sandwich.'

At which the three of us walk on.
The guard would as soon be doing this as something else.
He lights his pipe. Looks at his watch. It's almost time
for his lunch, and a glass of wine.
"Ask him," I say, "if he wants to be buried
in this cemetery when he dies.
Ask him where he wants to be buried."
My son is capable of saying anything.
I recognize the words *tombeau* and *mort*
in his mouth. The guard stops.
It's clear his thoughts have been elsewhere.
Underwater warfare. The music hall, the cinema.
Something to eat and the glass of wine.
Not corruption, no, and the falling away.
Not annihilation. Not his death.

He looks from one to the other of us.
Who are we kidding? Are we making a bad joke?
He salutes and walks away.

Heading for a table at an outdoor café.
Where he can take off his cap, run his fingers
through his hair. Hear laughter and voices.
The heavy clink of silverware. The ringing
of glasses. Sun on the windows.
Sun on the sidewalk and in the leaves.
Sun finding its way onto his table. His glass. His hands.

YESTERDAY, SNOW

Yesterday, snow was falling and all was chaos.
I don't dream, but in the night I dreamed
a man offered me some of his whiskey.
I wiped the mouth of the bottle
and raised it to my lips.
It was like one of those dreams of falling
where, they say, if you don't wake up
before you hit the ground,
you'll die. I woke up! Sweating.
Outside, the snow had quit.
But, my God, it looked cold. Fearsome.
The windows were ice to the touch
when I touched them. I got back
in bed and lay there the rest of the night,
afraid I'd sleep again. And find
myself back in that dream . . .
The bottle rising to my lips.
The indifferent man
waiting for me to drink and pass it on again.
A skewed moon hangs on until morning,
and a brilliant sun.
Before now, I never knew what it meant
to "spring out of bed."
          All day snow flopping off roofs.
The crunch of tires and footsteps.
Next door, there's an old fellow shoveling.
Every so often he stops and leans
on his shovel, and rests, letting
his thoughts go where they may.
Staying his heart.

Then he nods and grips his shovel.
Goes on, yes. Goes on.

WHERE WATER COMES TOGETHER WITH OTHER WATER

I love creeks and the music they make.
And rills, in glades and meadows, before
they have a chance to become creeks.
I may even love them best of all
for their secrecy. I almost forgot
to say something about the source!
Can anything be more wonderful than a spring?
But the big streams have my heart too.
And the places streams flow into rivers.
The open mouths of rivers where they join the sea.
The places where water comes together
with other water. Those places stand out
in my mind like holy places.
But these coastal rivers!
I love them the way some men love horses
or glamorous women. I have a thing
for this cold swift water.
Just looking at it makes my blood run
and my skin tingle. I could sit
and watch these rivers for hours.
Not one of them like any other.
I'm 45 years old today.
Would anyone believe it if I said
I was once 35?
My heart empty and sere at 35!
Five more years had to pass
before it began to flow again.
I'll take all the time I please this afternoon
before leaving my place alongside this river.
It pleases me, loving rivers.

Loving them all the way back
to their source.
Loving everything that increases me.

THE FIELDS

The worms crawl in,
the worms crawl out.
The worms play pinochle
in your snout.

Childhood ditty

I was nearsighted and had to get up close
so I could see it in the first place: the earth
that'd been torn with a disk or plow.
But I could smell it, and I didn't like it.
To me it was gruesome, suggesting death
and the grave. I was running once and fell
and came up with a mouthful. That
was enough to make me want to keep my distance
from fields just after they'd been sliced open
to expose whatever lay teeming underneath.
And I never cared anything for gardens, either.
Those over-ripe flowers in summer bloom.
Or spuds lying just under the surface
with only part of their faces showing.
Those places I shied away from, too. Even today
I can do without a garden. But something's changed.

There's nothing I like better now than to walk into
a freshly turned field and kneel and let the soft dirt
slide through my fingers. I'm lucky to live
close to the fields I'm talking about.
I've even made friends with some of the farmers.
The same men who used to strike me
as unfriendly and sinister.
So what if the worms come sooner or later?
And what's it matter if the winter snow piles up

higher than fences, then melts and drains away
deep into the earth to water what's left of us?
It's okay. Quite a lot was accomplished here, after all.
I gambled and lost, sure. Then gambled some more,
and won. My eyesight is failing. But if I move
up close and look carefully, I can see all kinds of life
in the earth. Not just worms, but beetles, ants, ladybugs.
Things like that. I'm gladdened, not concerned with
    the sight.
It's nice to walk out into a field any day
that I want and not feel afraid. I love to reach
down and bring a handful of dirt right up under my nose.
And I can push with my feet and feel the earth give
under my shoes. I can stand there quietly
under the great balanced sky, motionless.
With this impulse to take off my shoes.
But just an impulse. More important,
this not moving. And then
Amazing! to walk that opened field –
and keep walking.

SLIPPERS

The four of us sitting around that afternoon.
Caroline telling her dream. How she woke up
barking this one night. And found her little dog,
Teddy, beside the bed, watching.
The man who was her husband at the time
watched too as she told of the dream.
Listened carefully. Even smiled. But
there was something in his eyes. A way
of looking, and a look. We've all had it . . .
Already he was in love with a woman
named Jane, though this is no judgment
on him, or Jane, or anyone else. Everyone went on
to tell a dream. I didn't have any.
I looked at your feet, tucked up on the sofa,
in slippers. All I could think to say,
but didn't, was how those slippers were still warm
one night when I picked them up
where you'd left them. I put them beside the bed.
But a quilt fell and covered them
during the night. Next morning, you looked
everywhere for them. Then called downstairs,
"I found my slippers!" This is a small thing,
I know, and between us. Nevertheless,
it has moment. Those lost slippers. And
that cry of delight.
It's okay that this happened
a year or more ago. It could've been
yesterday, or the day before. What difference?
Delight, and a cry.

CIRCULATION

And all at length are gathered in.
Louise Bogan

By the time I came around to feeling pain
and woke up, moonlight
flooded the room. My arm lay paralyzed,
propped like an old anchor under
your back. You were in a dream,
you said later, where you'd arrived
early for the dance. But after
a moment's anxiety you were okay
because it was really a sidewalk
sale, and the shoes you were wearing,
or not wearing, were fine for that.

"Help me," I said. And tried to hoist
my arm. But it just lay there, aching,
unable to rise on its own. Even after
you said "What is it? What's wrong?"
it stayed put – deaf, unmoved
by any expression of fear or amazement.
We shouted at it, and grew afraid
when it didn't answer. "It's gone to sleep,"
I said, and hearing those words
knew how absurd this was. But
I couldn't laugh. Somehow,
between the two of us, we managed
to raise it. *This can't be my arm*
is what I kept thinking as
we thumped it, squeezed it, and

prodded it back to life. Shook it
until that stinging went away.

We said a few words to each other.
I don't remember what. Whatever
reassuring things people
who love each other say to each other
given the hour and such odd
circumstance. I do remember
you remarked how it was light
enough in the room that you could see
circles under my eyes.
You said I needed more regular sleep,
and I agreed. Each of us went
to the bathroom, and climbed back in bed
on our respective sides.
Pulled the covers up. "Good night,"
you said, for the second time that night.
And fell asleep. Maybe
into that same dream, or else another.

I lay until daybreak, holding
both arms fast across my chest.
Working my fingers now and then.
While my thoughts kept circling
around and around, but always going back
where they'd started from.
That one inescapable fact: even while
we undertake this trip,
there's another, far more bizarre,
we still have to make.

SCALE

for Richard Marius

It's afternoon when he takes off
his clothes and lies down.
Lights his cigarette. Ashtray
balanced over his heart.
The chest rising, then
sinking
as he draws, holds it,
and lets the smoke out in spurts.
The shades are drawn. His eyelids
closing. It's like after sex,
a little. But only a little.
Waves thrash below the house.
He finishes the cigarette.
All the while thinking
of Thomas More who,
according to Erasmus, "liked eggs"
and never lay with his second wife.

The head stares down at its trunk
until it thinks it has it
memorized and could recognize
it anywhere, even in death.
But now the desire to sleep
has left him, utterly.
He is still remembering More
and his hair shirt. After thirty years of wear
he handed it over, along with his cloak,
before embracing his executioner.

He gets up to raise the shades.

Light slices the room in two.
A boat slowly rounds the hook
with its sails lowered.
There's a milky haze
over the water. A silence there.
It's much too quiet.
Even the birds are still.
Somewhere, off in another room,
something has been decided.
A decision reached, papers signed
and pushed aside.

He keeps on staring at the boat.
The empty rigging, the deserted deck.
The boat rises. Moves closer.
He peers through the glasses.
The human figure, the music
it makes, that's what missing
from the tiny deck.
A deck no broader than a leaf.
So how could it support a life?

Suddenly, the boat shudders.
Stops dead in the water.
He sweeps the glasses over the deck.
But after a while his arms grow
unbearably heavy. So he drops them,
just as he would anything unbearable.
He lays the glasses on the shelf.
Begins dressing. But the image
of the boat stays. Drifting.
Stays awhile longer. Then bobs away.
Forgotten about as he takes up
his coat. Opens the door. Goes out.

ASIA

It's good to live near the water.
Ships pass so close to land
a man could reach out
and break a branch from one of the willow trees
that grow here. Horses run wild
down by the water, along the beach.
If the men on board wanted, they could
fashion a lariat and throw it
and bring one of the horses on deck.
Something to keep them company
for the long journey East.

From my balcony I can read the faces
of the men as they stare at the horses,
the trees, and two-story houses.
I know what they're thinking
when they see a man waving from a balcony,
his red car in the drive below.
They look at him and consider themselves
lucky. What a mysterious piece
of good fortune, they think, that's brought
them all this way to the deck of a ship
bound for Asia. Those years of doing odd jobs,
or working in warehouses, or longshoring,
or simply hanging out on the docks,
are forgotten about. Those things happened
to other, younger men,
if they happened at all.

The men on board

raise their arms and wave back.
Then stand still, gripping the rail
as the ship glides past. The horses
move from under the trees and into the sun.
They stand like statues of horses.
Watching the ship as it passes.
Waves breaking against the ship.
Against the beach. And in the minds
of the horses, where
it is always Asia.

THE GIFT

for Tess

Snow began falling late last night. Wet flakes
dropping past windows, snow covering
the skylights. We watched for a time, surprised
and happy. Glad to be here, and nowhere else.
I loaded up the wood stove. Adjusted the flue.
We went to bed, where I closed my eyes at once.
But for some reason, before falling asleep,
I recalled the scene at the airport
in Buenos Aires the evening we left.
How still and deserted the place seemed!
Dead quiet except the sound of our engines
as we backed away from the gate and
taxied slowly down the runway in a light snow.
The windows in the terminal building dark.
No one in evidence, not even a ground crew. "It's as if
the whole place is in mourning," you said.

I opened my eyes. Your breathing said
you were fast asleep. I covered you with an arm
and went on from Argentina to recall a place
I lived in once in Palo Alto. No snow in Palo Alto.
But I had a room and two windows looking onto the
      Bayshore Freeway.
The refrigerator stood next to the bed.
When I became dehydrated in the middle of the night,
all I had to do to slake that thirst was reach out
and open the door. The light inside showed the way
to a bottle of cold water. A hot plate
sat in the bathroom close to the sink.

When I shaved, the pan of water bubbled
on the coil next to the jar of coffee granules.

I sat on the bed one morning, dressed, clean-shaven,
drinking coffee, putting off what I'd decided to do. Finally
dialed Jim Houston's number in Santa Cruz.
And asked for 75 dollars. He said he didn't have it.
His wife had gone to Mexico for a week.
He simply didn't have it. He was coming up short
this month. "It's okay," I said. "I understand."
And I did. We talked a little
more, then hung up. He didn't have it.
I finished the coffee, more or less, just as the plane
lifted off the runway into the sunset.
I turned in the seat for one last look
at the lights of Buenos Aires. Then closed my eyes
for the long trip back.

This morning there's snow everywhere. We remark on it.
You tell me you didn't sleep well. I say
I didn't either. You had a terrible night. "Me too."
We're extraordinarily calm and tender with each other
as if sensing the other's rickety state of mind.
As if we knew what the other was feeling. We don't,
of course. We never do. No matter.
It's the tenderness I care about. That's the gift
this morning that moves and holds me.
Same as every morning.